THE ILLUSTRATED GUIDE

TO

heffield

AND

The Surrounding District,

𝕰𝖉𝖎𝖙𝖊𝖉 𝖇𝖞 𝕵𝖔𝖍𝖓 𝕿𝖆𝖞𝖑𝖔𝖗.

PRINTED AND PUBLISHED BY
PAWSON AND BRAILSFORD, SHEFFIELD.
1879.

First published in 1879 by Pawson and Brailsford.

This edition published in 2012 by ACM Retro Ltd.

ISBN 978-1-908431-18-9

www.acmretro.com

ACM Retro Ltd
The Grange,
Church Street,
Dronfield,
Sheffield S18 1QB.

Foreword

Look round the 21st century city and many of the key landmarks and buildings referred to in the 'Illustrated Guide to Sheffield' of 1879 are still very much in existence.

Weston Park Museum (complete with its star attractions, the Egyptian mummies); Bramall Lane Cricket Ground (it didn't become SUFC's home until a decade later); Glossop Road baths; Firth College (now the Leopold Hotel following many years as Sheffield Central Technical School) and the Hallamshire Savings Bank on Norfolk Street (now the Old Monk) have all stood the test of time in some shape or form.

Though life in Victorian Sheffield seems as far removed as you could get from modern day existence, there are more similarities than you think. The attraction of a trip to the country was as big back then as it is today.

Days out visiting Chatsworth, Haddon Hall, Hathersage or Castleton were very much in vogue.

Religion was obviously a huge part of Victorian life and the bulk of the churches featured in the 'Illustrated Guide to Sheffield' are largely unchanged and continue as places of worship.

One of the main absentees today is St Paul's Church - the grandiose building was demolished in 1937 to make way for the Peace Gardens.

Most of the other missing churches have the Sheffield Blitz of December 1940 to thank.

The first edition of the 'Illustrated Guide to Sheffield' was actually published in 1862 but many consider the 1879 version as the most visually stunning and appealing.

The full version spans over 560 pages with over 150 adverts. Our abridged version provides the highlights - complete with imperfections, the odd flaw and anything else you might expect as you re-introduce a Victorian masterpiece into the published world after 133 years.

The original book doesn't, unsurprisingly, spend much time trying to glorify the living conditions for the working classes. At that point in time there were thousands pouring into to the town to satisfy the labour demands of Sheffield's thriving steel trade.

The population at that point was around 200,000, it would be starting to nudge its present day level of 500,000 by the outbreak of WW1 - just four decades later.

It's interesting to note that the cult of celebrity was alive and kicking in Sheffield, even in 1879.

Though they weren't afforded brass plaques in the pavement outside the Town Hall as happens in the city today, they were given their own chapter in the book.

Poets, churchmen and scientists were the rock stars of the day. Faces such as poet James Montgomery, "Corn-Law Rhymer" Ebenezer Elliott and sculptor Sir Francis Chantrey were the head turners in Victorian Sheffield.

One name that has truly stood the test of time - murderer Charlie Peace who went on to be the subject of numerous books, films and magazines - obviously wasn't seen as high on the tourist trail list at that point, he didn't make the celebrity section.

Maybe they were still undecided about him - he was actually hung the same year as the guide came out.

Whilst many Victorians would have had their eye on happenings overseas, 150 soldiers had defended the Rorke's Drift supply station against 4,000 Zulu warriors in January 1879, there'd probably be no better place to peruse their heroic exploits than in the day's papers at the Sheffield Club on Norfolk Street. Described as "similar to the Clubs of London", it opened in 1862.

Sheffield of today, we firmly believe, is worse off for its absence.

We truly hope you enjoy our abridged 'Illustrated Guide to Sheffield' of 1879.

Neil Anderson.

SHEFFIELD

ROYAL VICTORIA HOTEL

Proprietress - MRS. GEORGE MEYER.

Honoured by the presence of their Royal Highnesses the PRINCE AND PRINCESS OF WALES on the occasion of their visit to this town.

FIRST-CLASS HOUSE,

Replete with every modern comfort, adjoining the Victoria Station, with which it is connected by a covered way.

VIEW OF SHEFFIELD FROM PARK HILL IN 1740.

The Guide to Sheffield.

E do not claim for Sheffield that the manufacturing parts are cleaner or less smoky than other similar centres of industry. The town has the reputation of being specially "black"—the railways which traverse the valleys where the large iron and steel works are concentrated, shewing travellers only its least attractive parts; but its extensive suburbs are remarkably beautiful, and perhaps no large town in the kingdom is situated in so charming and picturesque a district. In whatever direction we go beyond the outskirts of the town, a beautiful view is sure to meet the eye; and if the walk is extended four or five miles, delightful combinations of hill and valley, wood and stream, will be found, not to be surpassed except by the most lovely spots of Derbyshire or Cumberland. The town of Sheffield is situated in an amphitheatre of hills; many of the streets being steep, and some even precipitous. It used to be a boast that there was no street in the town from which the country could not be seen. This is no longer literally true; but large as the town has grown of late years, there are still very few localities from which glimpses of green hill-sides may not be obtained. The very spot on which the town stands must, centuries ago, have been one of the most lovely parts of a very beautiful district. The town is remarkably rich in names redolent of far-past times. " Daisy-walk," "Pea-croft," " Bower-spring," "Balm-green," " Figtree-lane," and other such names are suggestive of the primitive days, when birds warbled and fruits and wild flowers grew on what are now the most densely populated parts of the town; the now inky Don being then a pellucid stream, in which the most prized of fish so abounded that fields on its banks, since become the sites of large manufactories, were known as the " Salmon Pastures."

Sheffield is situated in the south of the West Riding of Yorkshire, on the borders of Derbyshire, and is about equidistant from the eastern and western coasts. It is on the eastern side of the range of lofty hills running southward from Westmoreland into Staffordshire, and often called the back-bone of England. The town is intersected by rivers, which add greatly to the natural beauty of the place, and also assisted in its early development as the great seat of the cutlery manufacture. There are five rivers which unite at the town—the Don, the Loxley, the Rivelin, the Porter, and the Sheaf, not inaptly compared by the poet Elliott to the "five fingérs of a hand." None of the rivers are large, the most considerable being the Don, of which the rest are tributaries; the Loxley and Rivelin uniting north-west of the town, and the Porter and Sheaf south-east, before their waters flow into the Don. It is generally supposed that the town derives its name from the Sheaf, which flows through some of the oldest parts of it; but a more recondite though less probable origin has been suggested.

THE PARISH OF SHEFFIELD.

The parish of Sheffield is ten miles long, extending from the townships of Tinsley and Handsworth, by which it is bounded on the east, to the lofty moorlands of Stanedge, where it terminates on the west. The eastern and more populous part is four miles wide; the western part is about half that width, narrowing to a point at Stanedge. The parish comprises five townships. Brightside Bierlow, the only township north of the river Don, is an irregular semi-circle in shape, having the river as its curved boundary, and extending beyond Grimesthorpe to the brow of Wincobank hill, where it joins the parish of Ecclesfield. The township of Sheffield is on the south side of the Don, and is flanked by Attercliffe-cum-Darnall on the northeast, and by Nether Hallam on the north-west. In addition to embracing the whole centre of the town—the site of "Old Sheffield"—the township of Sheffield stretches south-east over Park hill to Handsworth, and southwards to Bramall-lane and Heeley-bank. The township of Attercliffe is a triangle, of which Park-hill and the township of Tinsley form the two sides, with the Don as the base. Nether Hallam on the other side of the parish stretches southward from the Don to Crookes and Crosspool, having the Rivelin for its north-western boundary. Ecclesall Bierlow adjoins the township of Sheffield on the south, projecting into the town as far as the Crimean Monument at Moorhead, and the Union Inn at the top of Cambridge-street and Barker's Pool. It extends thence south-east to Heeley, and south-west to Broomhill, Tapton, and Crosspool. Ecclesall embraces nearly the whole southern and western suburbs, except Heeley and a part of Endcliffe, which are detached portions of Nether Hallam. It also extends over a considerable rural district lying between the Sheaf and the Porter, and stretching south-west a distance of four or five miles to Whirlow Bridge, Whiteley Wood, and Ringinglow. Upper Hallam, the only remaining and largest township, is chiefly agricultural and moorland, but includes the beautiful suburbs of Ranmoor and Fulwood, and the hamlet of Ringinglow. It extends from its junction with Ecclesall and Nether Hallam about due west to Stanedge, having the Rivelin for its northern and the Derbyshire moors for its southern boundary.

The acreage of the townships is as follows :—

Township	Acreage	
SHEFFIELD	3,436½	acres
ECCLESALL BIERLOW	4,180	,,
BRIGHTSIDE BIERLOW	2,680	,,
ATTERCLIFFE-CUM-DARNALL	1,336½	,,
NETHER HALLAM	1,902	,,
UPPER HALLAM	8,836	,,
	22,371	

This brief sketch of the extent and divisions of the parish of Sheffield seems necessary as an introduction to a brief sketch of its early history. We may add that the borough of Sheffield is co-extensive with the parish.

SUNDAY SCHOOLS.

THE WHITSUNTIDE GATHERINGS.

N very few towns are Sunday schools more largely and successfully carried on than in Sheffield. Such schools are conducted in connection with nearly all the churches and chapels of the different denominations; and in many instances the number of teachers and scholars is exceedingly large. One of the sights of the town on Whit-Monday, when the weather is propitious, is the gathering of teachers and children connected with the Sunday School Union. The Union is divided into four districts—the central schools assembling in Norfolk Park, those of the east branch in Firth Park, the west branch at Hillsbrough Park or some neighbouring place, and the Attercliffe branch at Attercliffe. The Union is composed of schools connected with the Congregational, Baptist, Presbyterian, Methodist New Connexion, Free Church, Primitive Methodist, and Wesleyan Reform denominations. The numbers at last year's gatherings were :—

	SCHOOLS.	TEACHERS.	SCHOLARS.
Norfolk Park	35	1,339	11,244
Firth Park	16	514	4,143
Hillsbrough	15	539	3,549
Attercliffe	12	341	3,316
Total	78	2731	22,252

The Wesleyan schools assembled at Wesley College and at Firth Park. The numbers last year were :—

	SCHOOLS.	TEACHERS.	SCHOLARS.
College	15	762	4,577
Park	9	334	2,719
Total	24	1,096	7,296

These gatherings take place about nine o'clock in the morning; the children having first assembled at their respective schools, had coffee and buns, and then walked in procession with banners flying to the general gathering places, where they form in circle and sing appropriate hymns. The number of spectators, is generally enormous, especially in Norfolk Park, where the spectacle is as gay as it is interesting and impressive —the children as a rule wearing their brand - new summer clothing for the first time.

A few of the Church schools meet in the Parish Church-yard. There is no general gathering of the rest. The usual mode of keeping Whit-Monday by the Sunday schools in connection with the Church of England is for the scholars to march round their respective parishes, with their banners, and then to attend a special service in their own parish church. There is also, in most cases, a treat given to the children in some private ground during the afternoon, and often a tea in the evening.

In the absence of any general census of Church Sunday schools it is impossible to give accurate figures, but the following estimate was made last year of the number of children and teachers belonging to Church schools within the Rural Deanery of Sheffield. Scholars, 16,930 ; teachers, 1,845.

The children of the Catholic schools, to the number of about 4,000, assemble to service at their respective churches in the morning, and spend the afternoon at Norfolk Park.

PUBLIC HALLS, &c.

HE CUTLERS' HALL, in Church-street, the splendid rooms of which are occasionally used for balls, dinners, and meetings of a more or less public character, we have already described on page 58. For township and district meetings, &c., the various Vestry Halls are let on easy terms.

THE ALBERT HALL, designed for musical entertainments and large public meetings, was opened on the 14th December, 1873, and is the property of a Joint Stock Company. It is centrally situated—but on a much too crowded site—at the junction of Barker's-pool and Burgess-street. The building is of red brick, relieved by granite pillars and carved stone cornice and tracings, but is remarkable rather for hugeness of appearance than for external beauty. The large concert room is 60 feet wide and 125 feet long. The organ, and an orchestra—arranged to hold 168 chorus singers, with band and soloists,—occupy one end. The saloon is the full width of the room and 103 feet long; and there is a two-tier balcony along the sides and across it, stalls behind the balcony at the west end, and a gallery above it. The saloon will seat 1,000 auditors, the balcony and stalls 700, and the gallery 500,—seats for a total of 2,200 persons, exclusive of the orchestra. The concert room is 50 feet high, the ceiling being hexagonal in shape, with a view to acoustic excellence, which has been most fully attained. Not the least attraction of the Albert Hall, in a musical sense, is the magnificent organ, erected by the celebrated French builder Mons. Cavaillé Coll, at a cost of £5,000. The case—from a design by Mons. Semil, a Parisian architect of eminence in this class of work — is of oak and Canadian pine. The organ is of immense size, having 74 stops and 4,064 pipes, is constructed with all the latest pneumatic and other improvements, and is in every respect admirably made. The perfection of its mechanism has excited the admiration of the English builders who have examined it. Not less marvellous is the instrument in respect of its immense power, the variety and exquisite clearness of its tones, and the grandeur of its combinations, which musical men agree in saying have seldom been equalled and probably never surpassed. It is unquestionably one of the best organs in the country. The Albert Hall was built at a cost (including the organ) of over £25,000. Alderman Fairburn is chairman of the Company. Mr. Joseph Peace, the secretary, has offices in the Hall.

MUSIC HALL.—The Music Hall, in Surrey-street, was erected in 1823, and belongs, like the Albert Hall, to a Company of Proprietors. The lower rooms are occupied by the Sheffield Library. Previous to the opening of the Albert Hall the large upper rooms were chiefly used for concerts, but are now occupied as a High School for Girls.

TEMPERANCE HALLS.—The Sheffield Temperance Society have a Hall in Townhead-street, which was built in 1855-6, at a cost of about £2,500. The principal room is 81 feet long by 51 feet wide, and, having a gallery at the end, will accommodate nearly 2,000 people. The Hall is let for lectures, political, trade, and other meetings and entertainments. There is a small Temperance Hall in Ellesmere-road.

FREEMASONS' HALL.—The Freemasons have a Hall at the corner of Surrey-street and Eyre-street, which, though not particularly handsome externally, is a building of which they have good reason to be proud. The Hall is the property of a Limited Liability Company, the shares in which are held exclusively by the several lodges and by individual members of the craft. The Freemasons purchased, in 1860, the building previously occupied by the Sheffield and Hallamshire Savings Bank, and some years later they also bought the adjoining house in Surrey-street. The new Hall was built upon the site of the old Savings Bank in 1876, and comprises banqueting room on the ground floor, and lodge room over it. The rooms are lofty, and are each 51 feet long and 26 feet wide. They are well built of stone, handsomely fitted and furnished, effectively warmed by hot water, and ventilated on the system recently patented by Mr. Tobin. The lodge room, which is particularly handsome, has an arched roof springing from a cornice, and ornamented with moulded ribs, panels, and carved bosses, the walls being relieved by columns with foliated capitals springing from ornamental corbels. There is a dais at the east end, reached by three steps ; a raised platform at the sides for a double row of chairs, and a fine-toned organ at the west end, built by Messrs.

Brindley and Foster. The lodge and banqueting rooms are approached by broad passages from the adjoining building, which comprises steward's room, kitchens, and lavatory on the ground floor, cloak and robing rooms on the first floor, and rooms for a resident hall-keeper on the second floor. The plans of Messrs. Scargill and Clark, the architects, provide for the rebuilding of this part of the property uniformly with the new Hall; and, when this has been done, the craft will have a suite of Masonic rooms second to none in the provinces as regards comfort, convenience, and elegance. The new Hall was formally opened by Sir Henry Edwards, Bart., Provincial Grand Master of West Yorkshire, July 18, 1877. There are four craft lodges in Sheffield—the Britannia, Brunswick, Wentworth, and Ivanhoe; two Royal Arch Chapters; a Rose Croix and a Mark Masons' Lodge, a Preceptory of Knights of the Red Cross of Rome and Constantine, and a Sanctuary of Knights of the Holy Sepulchre and St. John the Evangelist, together with a Priory of Knights of Malta.

THE ARTILLERY DRILL HALL, in course of erection, in Clough-road, for the use of the Artillery Volunteers, and described elsewhere, will be a valuable addition to the large rooms available for public gatherings and entertainments.

POST OFFICE, BANKS, NEWSPAPERS, PUBLIC COMPANIES, HOTELS, &c.

THE GENERAL POST OFFICE, at the top of Old Haymarket, was opened in 1872. It is a fairly handsome Doric structure, but inadequate to the requirements of the rapidly increasing postal and telegraphic business of so large a town. The building was intended for the accommodation of the Inland Revenue Department as well as postal business, but, in spite of the protests of the town, the Government declined to enlarge their plans, and had to rent offices in Norfolk-street, opposite the end of George-street, for the Inland Revenue Department, within a few months of the opening of the new building. A contribution towards the cost of the site was given by the town.

The town is well supplied with Branch Post Offices and Pillar Letter Boxes.

BANKS.—There are the following Banks in Sheffield:—
SHEFFIELD BANKING COMPANY, George-street (draw on Smith, Payne, and Co.), Mr. J. H. Barber, managing director, and

THE SHEFFIELD AND HALLAMSHIRE BANK.

Mr. E. Birks, manager; SHEFFIELD AND ROTHERHAM BANKING COMPANY, Church-street (draw on London and Westminster Bank, and on Barclay and Co.), Mr. Wm. Wild, manager; SHEFFIELD AND HALLAMSHIRE BANKING COMPANY, Church-street (draw on Glyn and Co.), Mr. A. Holdsworth, manager; SHEFFIELD UNION BANKING COMPANY, Bank-street (draw on Prescott and Co.), Mr. F. Stacey, manager; MIDLAND BANKING COMPANY LIMITED, Old Haymarket (draw on London and County Bank), Mr. G. Dawson, manager; LONDON AND YORK-SHIRE BANKING COMPANY LIMITED, 17, Old Haymarket (draw on Union Bank of London), Mr. A. C. Piggott, manager.

Several of the Banks have been greatly enlarged and improved, and are very handsome buildings. We give an illustration of the Hallamshire Bank, re-opened after its en-largement on the 1st of October, last year. It is a good speci-men of Greek Ionic of the severest order, and is a very fine building. The length of the façade, exclusive of the porch—

which is in a different style, being intended as the entrance to other buildings—is 71 feet 6 inches. The banking-room, which has an entrance at each end, is 60 feet long, 40 feet wide, and 34 feet high, with large dome in the centre. The interior decorations are in the Corinthian order, and are very beautiful. Mr. H. D. Lomas was the architect.

THE HALLAMSHIRE SAVINGS BANK.

THE SAVINGS BANK.—The Sheffield and Hallamshire Savings Bank, of which we give an illustration, is in Norfolk-street. It was established by subscription in 1819, the business being carried on at the Cutlers' Hall until 1832, and afterwards in Surrey-street. The present very beautiful edifice, built out of the surplus funds of the Bank at a cost of £5,500, was opened in June, 1860. The Bank is carried on under the supervision of fifty governors, among whom are many of the leading gentlemen of the town and neighbourhood. Its progress is shewn by the fact that the number of accounts has gradually increased from 265 in 1820 to 28,801 at the close of 1877, when the amount due to depositors was the large sum of £758,793, the investments amounting to £768,918, and leaving a balance in favour of the Bank of £5,124, exclusive of premises and furniture.

The Bank is open from 10 a.m. to 2 p.m. daily, and on Saturday evenings from 5 to 7. The rate of interest allowed on deposits is 3 per cent., and the formation of a Supplementary Investment Department enables the Bank to pay $3\frac{1}{2}$ per cent. on transferred deposits exceeding £50. Earl Wharncliffe is president of the Bank, and Mr. Frank Wever, actuary.

NEWSPAPERS. — There are three daily and three weekly newspapers published in Sheffield. The *Sheffield and Rotherham Independent* was established as a weekly newspaper in 1819, and since 1861 has been published daily, the weekly edition being also continued. Messrs. J. D. and R. E. Leader are the proprietors and editors of the *Independent* and of the *Star*, an evening newspaper. The *Sheffield Daily Telegraph* was established in 1855 as a daily morning journal; a weekly edition having also been published since 1861. Messrs. W. C. Leng and Co. are the proprietors and publishers, Mr. Leng being the resident manager and editor. The *Post*, a weekly paper, was established in 1872. Mr. Murphy is the proprietor and editor.

THE WATER COMPANY.—The Sheffield Waterworks Company have handsome offices in Division-street. Mr. Thomas Cockayne is chairman of the Company, and Mr. Walter Ashton, general manager. The extensive works of the Water Company are briefly described in a subsequent page, in connection with the disastrous flood caused by the bursting of the Dale Dyke reservoir.

THE GAS COMPANY.—The offices of the Sheffield United Gas Light Company are in Commercial-street, adjoining the General Post Office. They are most extensive, and admirably arranged, fitted, and furnished. The building is the handsomest and most imposing edfice of the kind in the town. The style is Early Renaissance. The harmony and extreme beauty of the design are so well shown in our illustration that a detailed description of the architectural features is unnecessary. Having a favourable site, the architects aimed to produce effect by grandeur of proportion and picturesqueness of outline, and in this aim, it must be admitted, they were eminently successful. The length of the façade is 131 feet. The stone used for facing is from Hallington, in Staffordshire, red Mansfield having been used for the pilasters. The pillars are granite monoliths, from the famous Ross of Mull. Messrs. Hadfield and Son were the architects. The Company carry on the business of gas fitting on a large scale, and have very extensive and hand-

THE GAS COMPANY'S OFFICES, COMMERCIAL-STREET.

some show rooms in connection with the offices. Mr. Fredk. Thorpe Mappin is chairman of the Company, and Mr. Thomas Roberts, general manager.

RAILWAY COMPANIES.—The main trunk line of the Midland Railway Company runs through Sheffield, connecting the town directly with the north and south of England, and with Scotland and South Wales. The Company are also the owners of the Rotherham Railway, and they have a special service to Doncaster, having running powers over the South Yorkshire Railway, from their Swinton station to that town. The Manchester, Sheffield, and Lincolnshire Railway furnishes ready access to Liverpool and other parts of the west coast, and to Grimsby, Hull, and the east coast. The alliance of the latter with the Great Northern Company secures to the town a second direct route to London and the South Eastern Counties. The South Yorkshire Railway—now leased to the Manchester, Sheffield, and Lincolnshire Company—gives the town a second important connection with Barnsley, Wakefield, &c., and with Goole, Hull, and the east coast, via Doncaster. The Midland Company have a commodious passenger station near Pond-street, on the site previously known as Sheaf Island. The three Companies have joint use of the equally large and commodious Victoria station.

TRAMWAY AND OMNIBUS ROUTES.—Tramways from the centre of the town to Attercliffe and Brightside were opened in 1876; and from Westbar to Hillsbrough and from Moorhead to Heeley and Nether Edge in 1878. On all these lines cars run every five or ten minutes. The Heeley and Nether Edge lines will eventually be continued to the centre of the town, and meantime an omnibus runs in connection with those tramcars from Moorhead to Old Haymarket. Omnibuses run at regular intervals between Old Haymarket and the Botanical Gardens, Broomhill, Ranmoor, Upperthorpe, and Pitsmoor suburbs, and also to Grenoside.

HOTELS.—In the olden days, when stage coaches were the great vehicles of travel, Sheffield was excellently provided for by the Tontine Hotel, erected in 1785, at a cost of £4,000 to £5,000. In 1850 the Tontine was sold to the Duke of Norfolk for £7,720, and taken down to make way for the Norfolk Market. The loss of this fine quadrangular hotel, with its large central yard and extensive accommodation, has never been thoroughly supplied, and is still spoken of with regret, in reference both to accommodation, and the intimate associations of the Tontine with "Old Sheffield." Of late years, however, the hotel accommodation has been greatly improved. The Royal Victoria Hotel, adjoining the Victoria Station, was built by a private company in 1862, at cost of £15,000. It is a large and very handsome structure. Among other leading Commercial and General Hotels are the Wharncliffe, King-street, with a large Restaurant and Public Dining-room; the Royal, Old Haymarket; the King's Head, Change-alley; the Angel, Angel-street; the Black Swan, Snig-hill; the Star and Clarence Hotels, High-street; the George, Market-place; the Imperial, Castle-street; the Brunswick, Old Haymarket; and many others. The projected street improvements are likely to lead to the erection of other large hotels, several being already projected.

COCOA AND COFFEE HOUSES.—A Cocoa and Coffee House, at Highfields, erected and furnished by Mr. F. T. Mappin, at a cost of about £4,500, was opened April 9, 1877. There are two large rooms on the ground floor in which tea, coffee, cocoa, and plain food are supplied, at exceedingly moderate charges. Over these are rooms for billiards, bagatelle, cards, dominoes, chess, and draughts, a small charge being made for the use of the billiard tables, cards, &c. Gambling and swearing in the rooms are prohibited. Newspapers and periodicals are provided for the coffee rooms. Cigars and non-intoxicant beverages are supplied in the billiard and card rooms. The rooms are open from 5.30 a.m. to 11 p.m. The house is well managed and is largely attended, and though established from philanthropic motives, is in fact self-supporting.

In 1877 a Café Company was formed, under the Limited Liability Acts, and has opened Cocoa and Coffee Houses in Gower-street, in the Wicker, at Attercliffe, in Castle-folds, and Mowbray-street. These houses are similar in character to that of Mr. Mappin's, and are also proving commercially successful. There are " British Workman" public houses in several parts of the town; a " Home" in Pea-croft; and a " Workman's Rest" in Pond-street, for the parish of St. Paul.

COMMERCIAL, LITERARY, AND OTHER PUBLIC INSTITUTIONS.

CHAMBER OF COMMERCE.—The Chamber of Commerce is a valuable institution, of which many of the principal manufacturers and merchants are members. It takes part in the discussion and direction of all questions affecting the trade of the town. Mr. W. K. Peace is president for the year, Mr. J. Nixon, secretary ; the offices being in East-parade.

THE SHEFFIELD CLUB is an institution for social purposes, similar to the Clubs in London. It is supported by the *élite* of the town, and carried on with great spirit. The Club House, in Norfolk-street, was opened in 1862 ; the style of architecture

THE SHEFFIELD CLUB.

being Palladian freely treated. In its erection, stateliness of appearance has been combined with the best internal arrangements. Every provision has been made for substantial comfort and for the amusements usual in such institutions. The cost of the building and fittings exceeded £7,000.

THE ATHENÆUM, which was established in 1847, occupies commodious premises in George-street, which were purchased and remodelled in 1859, and further improved in 1873. The building belongs to a Company of Proprietors, and is let free of rent, the condition being that four £5 shares shall entitle the holder to membership in, and all the advantages of, the Athenæum free of charge ; and one share, to the same privileges on payment of a yearly subscription of £1. The subscription for non-shareholders is £1 10s., and for ladies 10s. a year. The Athenæum combines the advantages of a Club with the addition of a commodious and well supplied newsroom and extensive library. The newsroom and library are on the ground floor, and also well furnished private rooms for the use of lady members. On the second floor is a large dining and coffee room and a club-room. Dr. M. Martin de Bartolomé is the president, and Mrs. Webster, librarian and secretary.

WORKING MEN'S CLUBS.—The movement for establishing Working Men's Clubs in Sheffield began in 1871. Ecclesall Club, adjoining South-street, Sheffield-moor, being opened in the early part of that year. Similar institutions were subsequently opened in other parts of the town. St. Peter's Club, held in the Old Council Hall, at the junction of Norfolk-street and Arundel-street, was opened in August, 1872. It has dining and coffee room, billiard rooms, reading, smoke, and club rooms, all of which are largely resorted to. Concerts and other entertainments are occasionally given on winter evenings. Refreshments of all kinds are supplied at the working men's clubs as at the more expensive clubs of the wealthier classes. Among the more successful suburban clubs are St. George's, Western-bank, and Highfield Club, London-road. The dinner is a much less important feature of these clubs than of St. Peter's, which has a crowded mid-day "ordinary," but members have the advantage of out-door recreation in the summer evenings. There are workmen's clubs at Attercliffe, Grimesthorpe, &c. Several of the clubs own the premises they occupy ; they are all fairly prosperous.

MEDICAL INSTITUTION. — The building belonging to this institution is situated at the end of Surrey-street, near Arundel-street. It was erected in 1829, and bears on the front the motto —"Ars longa, vita brevis." Dr. M. de Bartolomé is president, and Mr. A. Jackson, secretary.

LITERARY AND PHILOSOPHICAL SOCIETY.—This association was established in 1822, and numbers amongst its successive presidents many local men of distinction, socially or intellectually. Monthly meetings are held for the reading of papers, chiefly on matters of local interest. Lectures of a high class are occasionally delivered, and a conversazione of a very attractive character is annually held. The rooms of the Society are at the School of Art, in Arundel-street. Mr. H. C. Sorby, F.R.S., is president for the year; Mr. D. Parkes, librarian, and Messrs. B. Bagshawe and Edward Birks, secretaries.

CONSERVATIVE AND LIBERAL CLUBS.—The Conservatives have a central club and reading rooms in Furnival Chambers, Norfolk-street. The Liberals have a club in Angel-street.

SHEFFIELD LIBRARY.—This valuable institution belongs to a body of shareholders, and the Library contains about 80,000 books. The rooms are at the Music Hall, in Surrey-street. The shares are £5 each, and the yearly subscription £1 10s. Miss Manlove is librarian.

HIGHFIELD BRANCH LIBRARY.

FREE LIBRARY AND BRANCHES.—This institution is maintained by the Town Council, under the powers of the Free Libraries Act. The central Library, in Surrey-street, was opened in January, 1856, and branch Libraries were opened at Upperthorpe in October, 1869; at Burngreave-road in September, 1872; and at Highfield in August, 1876. The lower rooms of the Council Hall are used for the central Library, and new buildings have been erected for the branch Libraries from designs of Mr. E. M. Gibbs, of the firm of Flockton and Gibbs. The style of the Highfield and Upperthorpe Libraries is an adaptation of Italian, and the buildings are of red and white brick, with stone facings. They are handsome buildings, carefully fitted and adapted for their purposes, and well warmed and ventilated. They include capacious rooms for the lending and reference departments, and a general and ladies' reading room, both well supplied with magazines and periodicals. They are open daily (Sundays excepted) from 10 a.m. to 9.30 p.m. The large extent to which the Libraries are used is shown by the issues of books during the year ended August 31st, 1878. The volumes issued during the year were: From the central Library, 123,150; Upperthorpe, 80,861; Brightside, 82,989; Highfield, 69,410; making a total of 356,410, being 1,290 per day during the 276 days the Libraries were open. The Reference Department was open 284 days, and the number of volumes consulted was 26,964. The number of books at the end of the year was:—Central Library, 35,498; Upperthorpe, 9,266; Brightside, 9,189; Highfield, 6,858; total, 60,811. More than half the books issued from the Lending Departments are works of fiction, but the analyzed returns show an increasing demand for more solid works. The Free Library Committee propose to largely increase the stock of books, and to open new branches on a cheap but useful plan, as their funds permit. The Free Libraries are supported by a rate of 1d. in the £, which yielded £3,701 last year, and increases yearly.

THE ARMY AND THE VOLUNTEERS.

THE SHEFFIELD BARRACKS.—The Barracks at Sheffield are amongst the finest in the kingdom. They are situated on about 25½ acres of land, between the Penistone-road and the Langsett-road, in the outskirts of the town. They were finished in 1850. The front to Langsett-road is a handsome and imposing stone structure. There is a neat chapel at one end. The Barracks contain complete accommodation for a regiment of cavalry and an infantry regiment, and there are ample parade and drill grounds, &c.

THE VOLUNTEERS. — There are four different corps of Volunteers in the town, numbering altogether about 2,000 members. The several corps are maintained in a high state of efficiency, the Rifle, Engineer, and Artillery Volunteers having won distinction at several national gatherings of Volunteers for competition in drill and shooting.

YEOMANRY CAVALRY.—A local squadron of the First West York Yeomanry Cavalry has been in existence ever since the great French Revolution, at the close of the last century, and is still in a good state of efficiency. It consists of two troops, Mr. H. W. Verelst being captain of the A troop, and Mr. T. W. Jeffcock, of Shire House, of the B troop.

ENGINEERS.—The First West York Engineer Volunteers, established in 1859, in connection with the School of Art, has its head quarters in John-street, Highfield, and a bridging depôt near Hunter's-bar, Ecclesall-road. It consists of six companies, Lieut.-Colonel H. D. Lomas being the commanding officer.

THE HALLAMSHIRE RIFLES.—The Hallamshire Rifles (Second West York Rifle Volunteers) were established in May, 1859, the late Mr. Wilson Overend being the first commanding officer. The corps comprises a battalion of seven companies, the Earl of Wharncliffe being hon. colonel. ; Mr. T. E. Vickers, lieut.-colonel ; and Mr. Wm. Prest, major. The depôt is in Eyre-street, and the drill ground in Matilda-street.

ARTILLERY.—THE DRILL HALL.—The Fourth West York Artillery Volunteers, also established in 1859, consists of eight batteries, including those of Chapeltown and Handsworth. The corps have received four guns from the Government, and have a battery and magazine on Wadsley Common. The Duke of Norfolk is hon. colonel ; Mr. N. Creswick, lieut.-colonel ; Mr. Gillam Moseley, major. The present head quarters are in Tudor-street, but will shortly be transferred to Clough-road, where a very handsome drill hall, for their accommodation, is in course of erection, the foundation stone having been laid by the Duchess of Norfolk on the 25th September last, on the occasion of her first visit to the town. The plans provide for a lofty drill room, 180 feet long and 90 feet wide ; and a gun shed of the same length but narrower—the entrance being a lofty gateway, surmounted by a massive tower, and flanked by rooms for the officers and the administrative work of the corps. The estimated cost of the buildings is £9,000. The Duke of Norfolk has given £3,000, and the remainder is being raised in shares of £100 each under the Limited Liability Act, the promoters proposing to guarantee a dividend of 4½ per cent. The front buildings, chiefly of brick, will be in the Later Tudor style, the drill room having an iron roof in one span, on the model of St. Pancras station, London. It is proposed to let this room for dancing and other entertainments when not required for the purposes of the corps. Messrs. Hadfield and Son are the architects.

THE MONTGOMERY MONUMENT.

PUBLIC MONUMENTS, CEMETERIES, &c.

THE MONTGOMERY MONUMENT.—The memorial to James Montgomery, the poet, stands over his grave at the General Cemetery. It is near to the Cemetery-road entrance, the site commanding a beautiful view of the surrounding scenery. It was finished in July, 1861. This interesting memorial was in a large measure the work of the Sunday school teachers and scholars of Sheffield, who thus testified in the most practical way to the actively religious disposition of the departed bard as well as to his poetic fame. At the unveiling of the statue there was a public procession, in which the Town Council and all the local public bodies took part. The cost of the statue was £1,000. It was designed by Mr. John Bell, the eminent sculptor, and cast in bronze by the Coalbrook Dale Iron Company. It is a satisfactory work of art, and not unsuccessful as a likeness.

THE ELLIOTT AND SYKES' MONUMENTS.—The monuments to Ebenezer Elliott, "the Corn-Law Rhymer," and Godfrey Sykes, the artist, are described in our notice of Weston Park.

THE CRIMEAN MONUMENT.—A monument to the memory of the Sheffield soldiers and sailors who died in the service of their country in the Russian war in the Crimea has been erected at Moorhead. The foundation stone was laid by his Royal Highness the Duke of Cambridge. The monument is composed of Darley Dale stone and Aberdeen granite. The granite shaft is 18 feet long, the total height of the monument being about 58 feet. The Statue of Victoria, as "Honour," at the top, is nearly 10 feet high. From £1,300 to £1,400 was collected for the construction of the memorial, but a considerable portion was spent in preliminary expenses. Mr. G. Goldie, of London, was the architect, and Mr. Henry Lane, of Birmingham, the sculptor.

THE CHOLERA MONUMENT.—A neat and appropriate monument has been erected in Norfolk-road, opposite the Shrewsbury Hospitals, in memory of those who died in Sheffield from the ravages of the cholera in 1832, and who were buried on this spot. The disease raged from the beginning of July till the end of October. The numbers attacked were 1,347, of whom 402 died. Amongst the victims was Mr. John Blake, the master cutler. The monument was erected in 1834-5, the corner stone having been laid by Montgomery, the poet, in December of the former year.

CEMETERIES.—The burial grounds adjoining the churches having been most of them closed by the action of the Legislature, it has been necessary to construct Cemeteries outside the town. There was, however, one in existence previously to the closing of the old grave-yards, namely, the General Cemetery, opened in 1836, by a company of shareholders, who had at that time expended on it about £13,000. It then comprised about

THE CHOLERA MONUMENT.

six acres, but in 1848 about eight acres more were added, the total cost being about £25,000. It is situated at Sharrow, in the suburbs of the town, on a very beautiful spot. The Cemetery itself is most picturesque and tasteful in appearance, and contains monuments to many leading citizens, besides that of the poet Montgomery. There are two entrances, one in Ecclesall-road and the other in Cemetery-road. There is a handsome church in the Decorated style, with tower and spire, and also a chapel in the Doric order.

On the closing of St. Philip's Church-yard in 1857, a parochial burial ground was projected by the late incumbent, at the further extremity of the parish, on a dry and picturesque acclivity overlooking Birley Meadows and the vale of the Don. The Cemetery exceeds five acres in extent, and there is a neat mortuary chapel, vestry, and a lodge for the sexton. It is approached by the old road leading from Neepsend by the Club

Mill, and from Owlerton by a new road and bridge recently erected over the river Don. This burial ground was consecrated in 1859 by the late Archbishop of York. Riots occurred there in 1862, in consequence of an unfortunate exposure of dead bodies, improperly removed from their original resting places. The sexton's house, at Borough Lees, was fired by a mob, and the incumbent was afterwards prosecuted for some irregularity in the entries in the burial records. These events caused great excitement in the town during several weeks. The incumbent of St. Philip's officiates at the Cemetery, which, like the grave-yard round the church, is his freehold.

The Cemetery of the Brightside Bierlow district was constructed in 1859-60, on about 27 acres of land verging upon Burngreave-road, Pitsmoor, and the Occupation-road. The Cemetery was formed by the ratepayers, a Burial Board having been constituted for the purpose. The site cost £5,400, and about £11,600 has been expended in the laying out of the ground, the erection of mortuary chapels, and residences for the superintendent and head gravedigger, &c. The incumbents of Pitsmoor, the Wicker, Brightside, Neepsend, and All Saints' church conduct, in turns, the services in the consecrated part of the ground, and the Rev. J. Jefferson officiates on the unconsecrated side.

A Burial Board was also formed for the construction of the Attercliffe Cemetery, which is pleasantly situated, adjoining Christ Church, Attercliffe. It was consecrated in August, 1859; contains about six acres, and cost £1,332. The Board have spent a further sum of £968 in laying out the ground and building a neat chapel on the unconsecrated portion. The incumbent of Attercliffe is chaplain for the consecrated part, and the Rev. J. Calvert for the unconsecrated portion.

At Darnall a Burial Board has been formed and a Cemetery opened with an area of six acres. There are a church and chapel attached. The cost of land, buildings, &c., has been about £1,600. The vicar of Darnall is chaplain.

The Roman Catholics have a Cemetery at Rivelin Glen, a picturesque place on the north-western outskirts of the borough. It contains 4½ acres, and was opened in 1862, having been provided at a cost, including the erection of a neat Gothic church in the centre, of about £3,000. A new church was built last year, as mentioned in our account of the Catholic churches in the borough.

A public Cemetery for the township of Sheffield is in course of formation immediately beyond the Manor-lane, on the Intake-road. A Burial Board was elected in 1862, and proposed to provide a Cemetery near Darnall, making special arrangements with the Manchester, Sheffield, and Lincolnshire Railway Company for conveyance. The vestry rejected the proposal, and the project remained in abeyance for some years. In 1877 a new Board was elected, and purchased 50 acres of land from the Duke of Norfolk, at a cost of £13,625. The site extends from Intake-road, backwards up the hill towards Manor Lodge. It has been fenced round by a substantial stone wall, and contracts have been let for the erection of entrance lodge, board-room, offices, houses for the superintendent and sexton, and chapels for the Established Church and Nonconformists. The entrance to the Protestant part of the burial ground will be from Intake-road. A portion of the Cemetery—seven acres—nearest to the Manor will be appropriated to the Roman Catholics, the Duke of Norfolk providing the chapel and other requisite buildings for this part on plans to be approved by the Burial Board. The entrance to the Catholic burial ground will be from Manor-lane. The cost of the walling and of the offices, houses, and the Protestant chapels will be about £18,000, exclusive of roads, drains, and landscape work. The total cost, including the outlay of the Duke of Norfolk, will probably exceed £40,000. The Cemetery is within the township for which it is provided, the site being probably the best that could have been selected. The subsoil is dry and rocky, and there is an extensive view from the ground, of the south and west parts of the town and the moorlands beyond. There will be a chaplain for the unconsecrated part of the ground, the clergy of the various ecclesiastical parishes of the town providing for burial in the consecrated Protestant ground, and the Roman Catholic priesthood providing for burial in Catholic ground.

PUBLIC PARKS, GARDENS, &c.

WESTON PARK AND MUSEUM.—This pleasant place of public resort is in the western suburbs of the town, and has entrances from Western-bank and Winter-street. In July, 1873, the Town Council purchased Weston Hall, with the gardens and grounds (12a. 1r. 30p. in extent), from the execu-

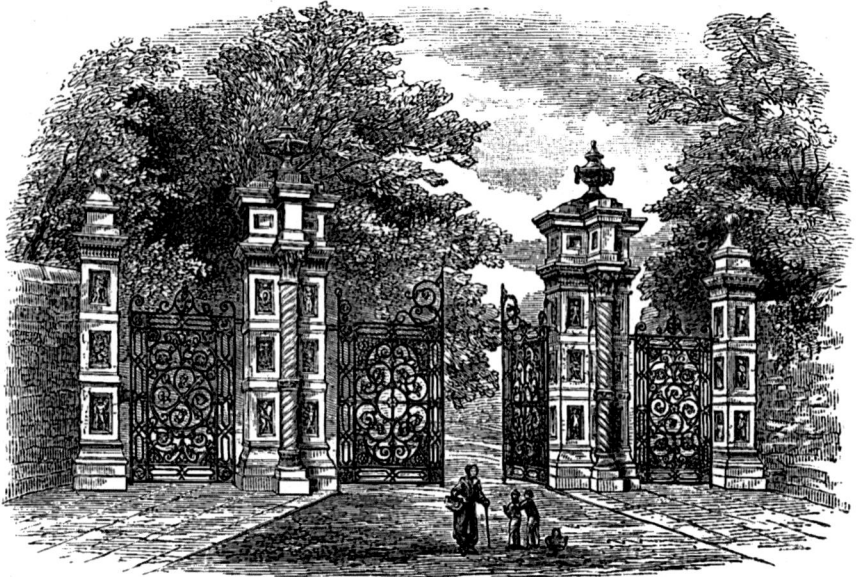

tors of the late Miss Harrison, for the purposes of a public
Park and Museum; the park being opened to the public May
4th, 1874, by the then mayor (Mr. Joseph Hallam). The
grounds, which have been greatly improved in conformity with
the designs of Mr. Marnock, landscape gardener, formerly of
Sheffield, have a bordering of fine trees, are adorned with
shrubberies, which improve every year, and are usually gay
with flowers in the summer time. There is a fountain at the
principal entrance; and a small lake in which are fish and
water-fowl under the trees on the north side.

There are interesting public monuments in Weston Park
in memory of Ebenezer Elliott, the poet and corn-law rhymer,
and of Godfrey Sykes, a local artist of reputation. Elliott's
monument is a bronze figure on a granite pedestal, the poet
being supposed to be seated on a rock in one of the spots so
charmingly described in his works. Mr. Burnand, of London,
was the artist. The monument was provided by public subscription in 1854, the cost being £600, and stood in the Market-
place until 1875, when a far more suitable abiding place was
found for it among the trees of Weston Park. The name
" Elliott " only is inscribed upon it.

The monument to Godfrey Sykes consists of a beautifully designed column in *terra cotta*, placed upon a pedestal of the same material. On one panel of the pedestal is a medallion portrait of the deceased artist, and on the opposite panel a representation of the working tools of his art. On the other panels are the following inscriptions:

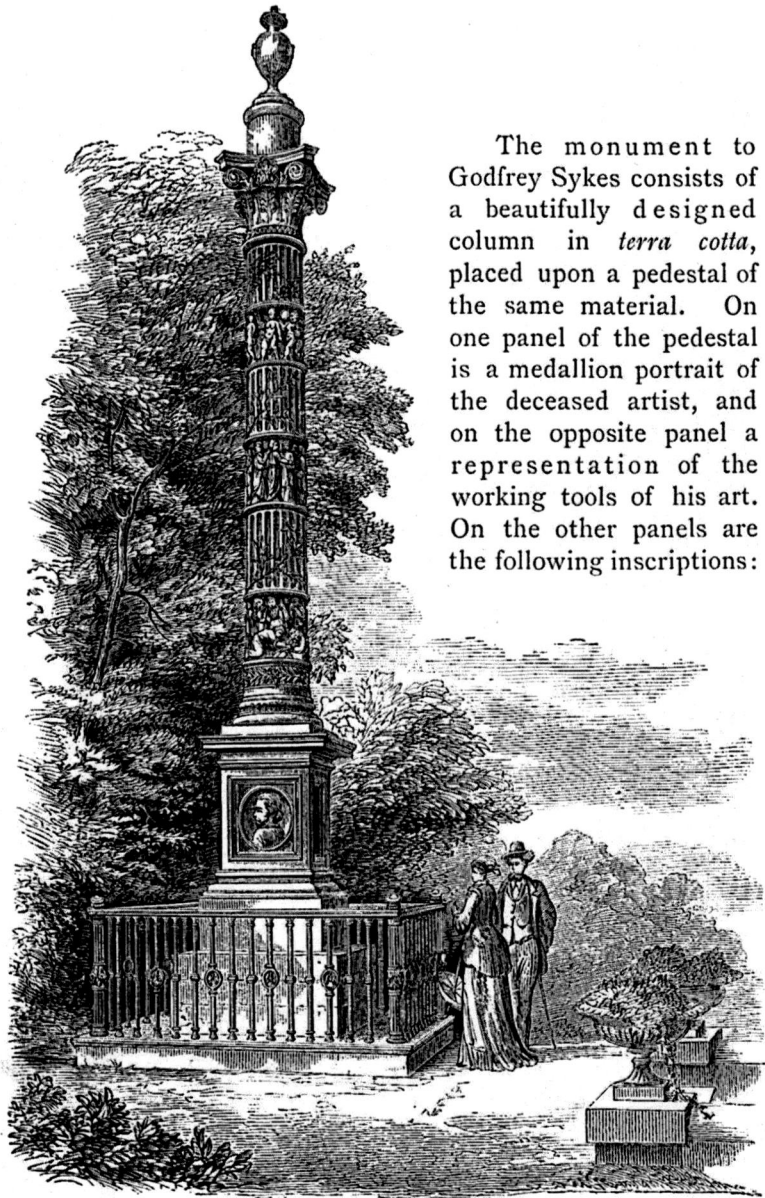

THE GODFREY SYKES MONUMENT.

"This monument was erected by the inhabitants of Sheffield in the year 1871, in memory of Godfrey Sykes. The column placed upon this pedestal is his work."

" Born at Malton in the year 1824 ; a pupil and afterwards master of the School of Art in this town ; he was called to London in the year 1859, to superintend the decorations of South Kensington Museum, and died there 1866."

The terra-cotta posts of the entrance gates, shown in our illustration, were composed from models executed by Mr. Sykes at South Kensington.

Seats are placed under the trees and beside the walks for the accommodation of visitors, and the park is a favourite place of resort, especially in the summer months.

The Picture Gallery and Museum, into which Miss Harrison's house has been converted, are also much visited. The exterior of the house has been preserved, but the partition walls of the principal rooms have been removed to make two large rooms, one in each story, 52 feet long and an average of 20 feet wide. In immediate communication with these are several smaller rooms, also parts of the old building. At the back two good art galleries have been built, each about 80 feet long and 25 feet wide. The rooms altogether are well arranged and lighted, and afford space for a considerable collection of works of art, manufacture, and other objects of interest. We are indebted to Mr. Howarth, the intelligent curator, for the following summary of the contents of the Museum :—

" The front room on the ground floor is devoted to the display of objects illustrating the processes connected with local manufactures. In the small room immediately adjoining this, and leading into the Natural History Gallery, are some very fine Greek and Etruscan antiquities, consisting of cinerary urns, vases, bronze vessels, personal ornaments, and'various domestic utensils. In the room corresponding to this on the front side of the building is arranged a rich collection of Egyptian antiquities, including the Egyptian portion of the Bateman collection. These antiquities comprise mummies ; numerous deities in bronze, wood, and porcelain; various ornaments and other objects. The Natural History Gallery contains collections illustrating zoology, geology, and mineralogy. Among the first is a very fine collection of Australian shells, numbering about 400 species, presented by Mr. J. Harris, per Mr. A. J. Mundella, M.P.; and a collection of European birds, formed by Mr. Henry Seebohm, F.R.S., and given by him to the Museum. The geological collection contains interesting remains of animals from the bone-caves at Cresswell Crags, Notts, and Castleton, Derbyshire. Only one side of the picture gallery is devoted to the display of pictures, which, with the exception of some portraits of local men, including Mr. Roebuck, M.P., Lord Brougham, and a few others (the property of the Museum), are all lent by local gentlemen. The remainder of the gallery contains the extensive collection of British antiquities (chiefly collected in Yorkshire and Derbyshire) formed by the late William and Thomas Bateman, and known as the 'Bateman collection.' This has been deposited in the Museum by its present owner, Mr. T. W. Bateman, of Middleton Hall, Derbyshire. The entire collection numbers about 4,000 objects, and is especially rich in antiquities of the Early British or Celtic period. There is also a good collection of Romano-British pottery, glass, bronze weapons and implements, leaden coffins, numerous fibulæ, armillæ, and other ornaments, as well as Anglo-Saxon, mediæval, and old English antiquities. A collection of more recent pottery, belonging to the Bateman collection, and including examples of Mayer, Wedgwood, Derby, Staffordshire and other wares, is exhibited in one of the upstairs rooms. Some fine examples of mediæval hammered iron work are suspended on the walls of the staircase. The upper floor contains a good collection of cutlery of various countries and periods, examples of Persian, Indian, and Japanese bronzes, chiefly contributed by Mr. William Bragge, F.S.A., who has been a liberal benefactor to the Museum. There is also an orrery, and a small general collection of ethnological objects, exhibited in these rooms."

A valuable observatory, presented to the Town Council by Miss Barker, daughter of the late Mr. Thomas Rawson Barker, is, we believe, about to be erected in Weston Park.

A residence has been erected for the curator at the Winter-street entrance. The cost of the original purchase was £18,750, and £4,000 to £5,000 more has been expended in alterations and additions and in improving the grounds. The sale of refreshments in the Park is prevented by restrictions in the will of Miss Harrison.

BOTANICAL GARDENS.—These gardens form one of the most attractive resorts in the neighbourhood. They are in the western suburbs, occupying about 18 acres of land between Clarkehouse and Ecclesall Roads, with entrances from both, the principal entrance being from Clarkehouse-road. They

CONSERVATORIES—BOTANICAL GARDENS.

slope down towards the valley of the Porter, and command picturesque views of the southern suburbs and the hills beyond. Sheltered by the high north wall is a noble range of conservatories, 340 feet long, containing many rare flowering and other exotics. The gardens were designed by Mr. Marnock, of Regent's Park Gardens, who was curator here for several years, and has since obtained great repute as a landscape gardener. They are laid out with great taste, and the summer displays of flowers are often quite gorgeous. They were provided by a company, and opened in 1836. The undertaking was not prosperous, and the company, after an expenditure of £18,000, was wound up in 1844, the gardens being sold to a new company of £5 shareholders. The number of shares is 1,800. The shareholders pay an annual subscription, and receive for each share a family ticket, which entitles the holder and his family to enter the gardens at all times when they are open. A proprietor of more than one share has the right of nominating a non-proprietor to the privileges of a family ticket in respect of each additional share. The subscription was 10s. 6d. until last year, when it was increased to 15s. 6d. Non-proprietors' tickets are sold at prices varying from 10s. 6d. to 21s. each. The only persons entitled to frequent the gardens are proprietors and nominees, including in all 1,800 families; but persons residing more than seven miles from the town are admitted as visitors on presenting a recommendation from a proprietor and entering their names in the visitors' book. Forms of recommendation are printed and issued to proprietors yearly, and are therefore readily obtained. On four gala days each season the gardens are thrown open to the public at a small charge. These galas are a considerable source of revenue, attracting many thousands of visitors when the weather is favourable. Alderman Grundy is chairman of the committee of management, Mr. Thomas Marshall, solicitor, St. James'-street, is secretary, and Mr. John Ewing, who resides at the gardens, is the curator.

ENTRANCE TO FIRTH PARK.

FIRTH PARK.—This park is part of the estate belonging to Page Hall, well known for many years as the residence of Mr. James Dixon (the founder of the celebrated firm of James Dixon and Sons, silver plate manufacturers) and subsequently of his eldest son, the late Mr. William Frederick Dixon, J.P. It is on the north-east side of the town, between Fir Vale, the residence of the late Mr. Edward Smith, and the village of Shiregreen. After the death of Mr. W. F. Dixon, Page Hall and the estate, consisting of 136 acres, were purchased by Mr. Mark Firth, who presented 36 acres of the estate to the town as a public park for ever. Two new approaches—one from the direction of Grimesthorpe, and the other from the Barnsley-road at Canon Hall, opposite the entrance to the new Sheffield Work-house—unite near the old entrance to the hall, and are continued in one road through the estate to the lane leading from the Barnsley-road, immediately beyond Brush House, to Shire-green. The park comprises a large part of the beautiful wood, 14 acres in extent, which formed the eastern boundary of the estate, and is on the right of the new road—also the open ground and smaller wood on the left beyond Page Hall. This latter part extends over the hill to the boundary of the Bolsover and Brush House estates. One portion of the park is appropriated for games; the other portion, which is more undulating, being intersected with winding walks and diver-sified with shrubberies and flower beds. Along the edge of the small wood is a pleasantly-shaded ridge from which there is a wide view of a charming landscape, with a glimpse between the Wincobank and Osgathorpe hills of the tall chimneys of the Don valley as a background. Walks have also been made through the larger wood, and no restraint is put on visitors, who may wander over the park and through the woods at will. Mr. Firth made the new approaches to the park and the excellent carriage-drive through it at his own cost, erecting a handsome lodge and refreshment rooms at the entrance. The park is some two miles north of the central parts of the town, and the roads over the Pitsmoor and Osgathorpe hills are steep; but it is near the increasing population of the Don and Grimesthorpe valleys, to whom, as the town extends, it must become an immense boon. The park was publicly opened August 16th, 1875, by the Prince and Princess of Wales, who were guests of Mr. Firth, at Oakbrook, for several days. Some account of the royal visit will be found elsewhere. We may add that there is a footpath across the fields from Firth Park to the old British camp at the summit of Wincobank hill. The distance is less than half-a-mile; and the camp, of which some notice will be found in our account of ancient earthworks, is worth a visit for its own sake as well as for the view from its vallum of the Don valley to Rotherham and the wide expanse of country beyond.

NORFOLK PARK.—This park, situated on the estate of the Duke of Norfolk, the town owes to the munificence of the grandfather of the present inheritor of the title. The park com-prises altogether more than 60 acres. It has been laid out in ornamental walks, carriage drives, &c., and is well planted with shrubs and trees. In the centre there is a large open space covered with grass, which is used for cricket matches, &c. Very beautiful views of the surrounding scenery may be obtained from various spots in Norfolk Park. The park was commenced in 1841 by Duke Bernard Edward, and completed by his successors. Though dedicated to public use, it remains the property of the Duke of Norfolk, and is kept in order at his expense. There are two entrances—one of them from Norfolk-road, a short distance beyond the cholera monument, and the other from Belle Vue-road, which divides the park from the Farm, the Sheffield residence of his Grace. A new approach to the Norfolk-road entrance has recently been made from Suffolk-road, near the Midland railway station.

St. George's Museum.—This unique and interesting museum, founded by Mr. John Ruskin, the eminent writer and art critic, is at Upper Walkley, in the north-western suburbs of the town—close to the district where, through the instrumentality of freehold land societies, so many of the more thrifty artizans have provided themselves with homes on their own freeholds. Mr. Ruskin purchased an acre of land with a good stone cottage upon it several years ago, and uses the principal room in the cottage for the museum. This, however, is a temporary arrangement. New buildings are to be erected, and are to include a picture gallery, library, and reading room. The contents of the museum at present are: 1. A small but rich and rare mineral collection, containing some of the finest specimens of precious stones the country possesses. Probably nowhere else in Europe can so valuable a collection be found in so small a space as is contained in Mr. Ruskin's cabinet at Walkley. 2. A natural history section, composed not of stuffed specimens out of which all the life has gone, but of the best illustrated works published, many of them containing original drawings of great beauty and value. 3. A botany section, composed of carefully executed drawings, some of the most beautiful being Mr. Ruskin's own work. 4. A small collection of paintings and drawings, chiefly from the old masters; a few of them originals of great value, the rest careful copies and studies of the best works. 5. A small collection of classical literature, Greek, Latin and English, all valuable, and some of them rare old works and splendid specimens of typography. There are also a few busts and other studies. The St. George's

Museum is not intended for the recreation of mere sight-seers—
though visitors are freely admitted—but as an educational
institution for art students. The collections are carefully
arranged with a view to progressive study; clear and exact
instructions in drawing from Mr. Ruskin's own pen being
supplied for the guidance of elementary students. The number
of students is from forty to fifty, some of them living at a
distance, and coming to the town for a few weeks at intervals.
An exceedingly valuable museum will ultimately be formed.
It will not be large but choice, the aim of the founder being to
provide at Walkley a perfect type of museums to be established
in various parts of the country, for the cultivation of art in its
truest and best forms. Mr. Ruskin and a number of gentlemen associated with him, desire to place within the reach of
the humblest artizan, with a taste and capacity for art, as
perfect an educational museum as the wealthiest student can
command. As the result of the opportunities opened to him
at Walkley, one youthful Sheffield grinder is already on the
high road to artistic eminence, and others of the most labo-
rious students are artizans. The museum is on the slope of
the hill overlooking the Rivelin valley, and commanding extensive and beautiful views of the country beyond. The easiest
access from the centre of the town is by the Hillsbrough
tramway car to the foot of Greaves - street, or the Walkley
omnibus to Spring-vale, the walk from either point being less
than half-a-mile. The nearest way from the west end of the
town is by the new road immediately below Cobden-view to
the old lane from the village of Crookes to Heavygate-road.
A field-path from this lane over Bole-hill, from which there are
very fine views, terminates in Walkley-lane, within 100 yards of
the museum. The museum is open to students daily (Thursdays
excepted) free of charge. Visitors may obtain tickets from Mr.
Thomas Rodgers, Market-place, or by letter from Mr. Swann,
the curator.

RECREATION GROUNDS.—The Duke of Norfolk has presented to the town plots of land in three populous neighbour-
hoods—Parkwood-springs, Carlisle-street east, and Bacon-lane,
Attercliffe—for permanent Recreation Grounds. The plots,
amounting altogether to 26 acres, are being levelled and fenced
at the joint expense of his Grace and the Town Council.

BOWLING GREENS.—There are seven bowling greens in the
town, most of them the property of shareholders and maintained

by annual subscriptions. The oldest of these greens is in Broomgrove, and was established in 1851. It is exclusively proprietary, and numbers among its one hundred members some of the leading magistrates and other gentlemen of the town. The Norfolk Bowling Green adjoins the Bramall-lane cricket ground, and is large and well-formed. There are good bowling greens very pleasantly situated at Pitsmoor, Steel-bank, Nether-edge, East-bank and Heeley.

CRICKET AND FOOTBALL.—The public Cricket Ground is in Bramall-lane, the land being leased from the Duke of Norfolk. It was opened in 1855, at a cost of nearly £3,000. The ground is under the management of a committee of proprietors. This committee have organized a large county club for the promotion of cricket, the annual subscription to which is a guinea a year, which, however, is called for only when required. The subscribers are chiefly gentlemen living in Sheffield and the neighbourhood. As the result of this organization, a number of leading county and other interesting matches are played every season on the Bramall-lane ground, and attract many thousands of spectators; and Sheffield has become the real centre of county cricket in Yorkshire. The affairs are managed with judgment and spirit. The ground has been freed from heavy responsibilities during the last few years, enlarged and improved, and the committee have now (1879) a considerable fund in hand to meet future contingencies. The area of the ground, since the enlargement in 1875, exceeds ten acres. Many of the cricket clubs of the town practise on the Bramall-lane ground; others have private grounds in the suburbs.

FOOTBALL CLUBS.—Football is a popular game in Sheffield, most of the clubs renting fields for practice. These clubs have annual sports and athletic games, some of which are largely attended, the sports of the Sheffield and other leading clubs attracting the *élite* of the town.

BICYCLE CLUBS.—During the last few years bicycle riding has become a favourite amusement, and several clubs have been formed. Some of the principal clubs have a practice ground at Sharrow-vale. The members have occasional excursions, often riding great distances over the hills which hem in the town on all sides.

RACES AT SHEFFIELD.—There were races at Sheffield as far back as 1713, when, it is recorded, the Town Trustees were "At charges to get horses to the races." At what date they were established is not known. The race-ground was at Broom-hill, the grand stand being on the site now occupied by Stand House, Fulwood-road. The site was part of Crookesmoor, the enclosure of which, under the Act of 1779, put an end to the races. Repeated attempts have been made of late years to re-establish races at Sheffield. In 1875, a Limited Company was formed for the purpose, with a capital of £15,000, sub-scribed chiefly by professional sporting men. The Company purchased a freehold site of about 100 acres, adjoining the road to Redmires and about 4½ miles from the town. This, having been enclosed and provided with suitable buildings, was opened as a race ground, and several meetings took place. The races did not attract the attention of leading sportsmen to any con-siderable extent, and have been discontinued. There are several foot-racing grounds in connection with public-houses : they attract the working-classes and promote betting and neg-lect of work to an extent which makes them a serious evil.

THEATRE ROYAL.—The Theatre Royal is at the corner of Arundel-street and Tudor-street, and belongs to a Company of Proprietors. It was erected in 1773, and was rebuilt in 1854-5, with the exception of the outer walls, at a cost of £3,000.

ALEXANDRA THEATRE.—The Alexandra Theatre is in Blonk-street. It was originally built for equestrian perfor-mances, but on the destruction of the Surrey Music Hall, Westbar, by fire in 1865, it was opened as a theatre and concert room by the late Mr. Thomas Youdan. Mr. William Brittlebank is the lessee.

THE SOUTH YORKSHIRE LUNATIC ASYLUM.—At Wadsley Park, a short distance beyond the northern boundary of the borough of Sheffield, a very large Lunatic Asylum has been erected for the West-Riding. The extent of the grounds is 163 acres. The original buildings consist of three large blocks. The administrative block is in the centre, and comprises Visiting Justices' and general rooms, kitchens, dining hall, store rooms, officers' quarters, &c. Springing out of the central building is an elegant clock-tower of stone 96 feet high, and elaborately ornamented. Communicating with the central block by wide corridors, are large east and west wings ; the former are for the male lunatics, and the latter for the women, — the two wings containing accommodation for 800 patients. Behind the centre block are brewery, corn mill, bakehouse, &c., all on a large scale, fitted with steam machinery. Behind the women's quarters is an extensive laundry, also fitted up with machinery, and having large drying ovens heated by steam. South of the main buildings, but at some distance, is the church, a considerable and very handsome stone edifice. These buildings constituted the Asylum as opened in 1872. Two additional wings have since been built, and the Asylum now contains accommodation for 1,600 patients. The material used in the building is red pressed brick, made on the ground, with stone facings. The institution at Wadsley is considered to be one of the finest Pauper Lunatic Asylums in the country. It certainly comprises a very imposing group of buildings, in the construction and fitting up of which no necessary expense has been spared. The machinery and fittings in every department are of the most improved kind. The capacious kitchens are models in regard both to general construction and apparatus. There are extensive farm buildings on the estate, and the lunatics, principally the men, are largely employed in farm and garden work, the land being kept in a high state of cultivation, and supplying the needs of the institution in fruits, vegetables, and cereals. Much of the general work of the institution is also performed by the lunatics—the men being employed in brewing, grinding, baking, &c., and the women doing the laundry and other such work. The men have, moreover, done much of the brick-making and other work in connection with the newer buildings. In front of the buildings are extensive lawns, flower gardens, and shrubberies, in which lunatic labour is also largely utilized. Copious springs on the estate supply the huge institution with water. In the course of the excavations for the buildings a very interesting geological discovery was made. The stumps and roots of several large trees petrified by long exposure to undercurrents of water into hard mineral stones were found. They are preserved under cover and shown to privileged visitors. Dr. S. Mitchell is the resident medical superintendent of the Asylum, and Mr. Pigott is the steward.

FEVER HOSPITAL.—A Fever Hospital is in course of erection by the Town Council on an elevated site adjoining Winterstreet. The site contains 6,695 square yards, and the Hospital is in blocks, on what is known as the "Pavilion" plan. There are two detached blocks on each side of a parallelogram; the administrative block, also detached, being at the further end of the square. The buildings, which are of brick with stone dressings, have two stories, with windows on both sides. In each block there are two rooms, one on the ground floor and one above, each large enough to contain eight beds, with adjoining rooms for nurses, the latter having projecting octagonal ends, with a view to complete external ventilation. The Hospital will contain accommodation for 64 patients, sixteen in each block. The architect is Mr. S. L. Swann, of George-street, the plans having been selected by the Health Committee, under the advice of Captain Galton, C.B., in an open competition. The cost of the buildings, exclusive of furnishing, will be about £15,000, and the cost of the site was £1,750.

BATHS.—The Town Council erected public Baths in Corporation-street in 1870, at a cost of about £3,000, and they are largely patronized. They are now providing commodious Baths near the junction of the Tinsley and Newhall-roads, at Attercliffe, from designs prepared in the Borough Surveyor's Office.

THE SHEFFIELD BATH COMPANY Limited have established swimming, Turkish and other Baths in Convent-walk, Glossop-road. The buildings, from designs of Mr. E. M. Gibbs, are lined throughout with glazed bricks, and embrace two swimming Baths, the largest of which is 70 feet by 30 feet, Turkish Baths, reputed to be the best arranged and most luxurious in the kingdom, and many other descriptions of Baths.

THE NORFOLK BATHS are situated in Bramall-lane. The large swimming Bath measures 75 feet by 39 feet.

THE SHEFFIELD TURKISH AND PUBLIC BATH COMPANY Limited have commodious Turkish and other varieties of Baths in Union-street.

THE PUBLIC MARKETS. — The Markets of the town are under the control of, and the buildings in which they are held belong to, his Grace the Duke of Norfolk, as Lord of the Manor. Of late years the town has outgrown its Market accommodation. Negotiations have taken place between the Council and the Duke with a view to the purchase of the Markets for the town. The negotiations failed on the question of price, and a large and much-needed extension of Market accommodation is being made at the expense of his Grace.

NORFOLK MARKET HALL.—The Norfolk Market Hall, of which we give an illustration, was opened at Christmas, 1851, occupying the site of the old Tontine Hotel. The entire cost of the erection, inclusive of site, was something approaching £40,000. It is built in the Tuscan style, of brick, with stone basements, quoins and dressings. It is 296 feet long, 115 feet

wide, and 45 feet high in the centre. The building, which contains a large fountain, is divided into stalls and shops for the sale of fruits, vegetables, confectionery, and a great variety of wares.

THE NEW CORN EXCHANGE.—There is a weekly corn market at Sheffield, held on Tuesday. For many years the corn factors who frequented the Sheffield market assembled at the upper end of the Shambles and transacted their business in the open air. A corn exchange was built in 1830, but has become much too small for the requirements of the trade since the town became an important railway centre. It has been felt for some time that if adequate accommodation were provided, Sheffield, from its central situation, must soon become one of the most important corn markets in the kingdom. Several schemes for that purpose were proposed during the minority of the present Duke of Norfolk, but it was not until the Duke came into possession of the estates that the work was actually undertaken. Acting upon the advice of his agent, Mr. Ellison, that an alteration of the present buildings was inexpedient, his Grace gave instructions for the erection of a new exchange on the further side of the market; being, in fact, the site on which the original Shrewsbury Hospital formerly stood. Designs have been prepared by Messrs. M. E. Hadfield and Son, and the work is already in progress. The new structure will comprise the Corn Exchange, which will occupy the centre of the pile of buildings, being, really, a covered court with four entrances, one in each façade. It will be 150 feet long by 75 feet wide, having the open roof so arranged as to admit a north light. It will be in five spans, supported by pillars of Hopton Wood-stone, and having arched principals. There will be a series of five three-light windows to the east, and the settling rooms, retiring rooms, &c., are all conveniently placed. The principal façade of the building fronting the old Corn Exchange will be 224 feet in length, and the fronts to Broad-street and the Canal Warehouse 135 feet. On the ground floor on each side of the entrances will be an arcade, in which there will be sale shops. At the north-west corner will be a commercial hotel and restaurant on a large scale. The Norfolk estate offices will occupy the chamber floor of the south and west wings, and on the east front will be shops and offices for wharfingers, &c. The whole structure will be cellared. The design of the exterior of the building, as seen in our illustration, is of the Late Pointed or Tudor type, the materials being thin red bricks of the best description, and stone facings from the Bole Hill quarry, near Treeton; the roofs being covered with Broseley tiles. In the centre of the

NEW CORN EXCHANGE.

principal front will be a massive tower, through which the great hall will be approached by a flight of ten steps; the ceiling will be vaulted in stone; and there will be right and left entrances to the estate offices and suites of chambers. Above this vaulted gateway will be constructed a spacious fire-proof muniment-room, approached from the estate offices, for preserving the deeds and records of the Norfolk estate at Sheffield. It is expected that the whole will be completed in about two years from the present time. It will be a very noble and commodious building.

A wholesale fruit and vegetable market is held daily on the covered space between Norfolk Market and the old Corn Exchange.

The Norfolk estate offices are at present in the old Corn Exchange, where they will remain until the opening of the new Exchange. Mr. M. J. Ellison is the agent of his Grace.

A fat cattle market is held on Mondays, and a general cattle market on Tuesdays, on the open ground between the approach to the Victoria Station and the River Don.

There are two fairs annually—one in Whit-week and the other at Christmas. These are held on the usual market grounds. They are now chiefly pleasure fairs.

The Fitzalan Market extends from Market-place to Old Haymarket. The building includes butchers' shops, poultry and fish market.

During the last few years vast improvements have been made in the shop architecture of the town as in public and commercial buildings generally. Many large and handsome buildings have already been erected. As the comprehensive schemes of street improvement undertaken by the Corporation and the Town Trustees are carried out, the number of such buildings will rapidly increase, and Sheffield will possess central streets rivalling in width and in the beauty of their architecture those of the best towns in the provinces. As a specimen of this class of buildings we give an illustration of the large establishment of Messrs. Cole Brothers, which occupies a commanding position opposite the Parish Church. The building, which is being greatly enlarged, is an irregular square, having a frontage of 86 feet to Church-street, 94 feet to Fargate, and a corner frontage of 20 feet, in which is a main entrance, towards High-street. It is built in the Modern French style of architecture,

MESSRS. COLE BROTHERS, CHURCH-STREET AND FARGATE.

and has five stories. Sir Gilbert Scott, when visiting the town
a few years ago, spoke of it as "the best example of shop
architecture" he knew. Messrs. Flockton and Gibbs are the
architects.

EDUCATIONAL INSTITUTIONS.

HE GRAMMAR SCHOOL.—Thomas Smith, an attorney at Crowland in Lincolnshire, a native of Sheffield, may be looked upon as the founder of the Grammar School. The wording of the early documents is curious. In 1603, the founder bequeathed to the town of Sheffield £30 a year, "so long as the world should endure, for the finding of two sufficiently learned men to teach and bring up the young children there in godliness and learning, that is to say, a schoolmaster and usher, the former of whom was to receive £20 per annum and the latter £10, to be elected by the minister and twelve of the best and most sufficient parishioners of Sheffield, and by them to be removed at pleasure." In 1604, King James, on the application of the inhabitants, granted letters patent for the establishment of the School. The letters patent declare that the King erects, creates, founds and establishes a school in the town of Sheffield for the education of the youth of that town and parts adjacent, to be called " The Free Grammar School of King James of England, within the town of Sheffield, in the County of York," and to consist of one pedagogue or master, and one sub-pedagogue or usher, and of the children and youth therein taught and instructed. They incorporate the vicar and twelve principal inhabitants as governors, vesting the Trust property in them and also the election of master and usher, with a power of removal at pleasure ; require that the master shall be an M.A. or B.A. at least, and that he and the usher must instruct the scholars in Latin and Greek letters ; and they direct the governors to apply the profits of the lands, &c., settled on the School, " to the relief, sustentation and maintenance of the master, usher, and scholars, and the " sustentation and reparation " of the School house and other messuages on the School estates. The Church Burgesses granted the governors a school house, with garden and croft, at a nominal rent, and in 1648 a new school house was built " with materials from the Sheffield Castle." That School was in Townhead-street. The present School is a good stone structure in St. George's-square, and was erected by public subscription in 1824. Property was left to the School by other benefactors from time to time, and the income now amounts to about £200 a year ; but this is in-

COLLEGIATE SCHOOL.

sufficient to constitute a "Free Grammar School" according to the terms of the original charter, and the only advantage to the town is that the masters are required to teach about thirty boys at half the ordinary charge. The School is open to all religious denominations. Mr. J. E. Jackson, M.A., D.C.L., is head master, and Mr. W. Doig, M.A., second master.

THE COLLEGIATE SCHOOL.—This institution is situated at Collegiate-crescent, Broomhall Park, and was established to provide a thoroughly sound education for the youth of the upper classes, preparatory to a University course or to commercial pursuits. It cost nearly £10,000; the school house, which is a handsome building in the Tudor style, having been erected in 1835, Lord Wharncliffe laying the first stone. There are 3½ acres of pleasure grounds, tastefully laid out, and a commodious residence for the principal and for the reception of boarders. The building is situated in a picturesque part of the suburbs, outside the smoke and bustle of the town. The Rev. James Cardwell, M.A., is the principal. The house contains accommodation for forty boarders. In connection with the School are scholarships amounting to £300 a year.

WESLEY COLLEGE.—Wesley College is a large and handsome stone building, situated in Glossop-road, belonging to the Wesleyans, and occupied as a high-class school. It has ample grounds, a southern aspect, and commands extensive views of picturesque scenery. The site contains 5a. 2r. 26p., and was purchased in 1836 for £4,218. The centre part of the College was built first, and opened August 8th, 1838. The large school-room, forming the eastern portion, was added in 1839; and the chapel, at the west end, in 1840. The original cost of the site, buildings, and furniture was £27,696. The late Mr. W. Flockton was the architect. The building was suggested by the late Rev. S. D. Waddy, one of the Wesleyan ministers stationed in Sheffield in 1835. The funds were raised by the issue of £50 shares to leading Wesleyans in Sheffield and other places, and the institution, intended to supply a classical and superior general education, was at first called the Wesleyan Proprietary Grammar School. In 1844, Dr. Waddy, the original promoter, was appointed governor and chaplain—a position he held until 1862. Soon after his appointment, an application was made to Sir James Graham, and a Royal Warrant was issued, constituting the School a College of the University of London, and empowering it to issue certificates to candidates for examination for the several degrees of Bachelor and Master of Arts, and Bachelor and Doctor of Laws. The College contains accommodation for 225 inmates. It is not restricted to sons of Wesleyans, and has been from the first a prosperous institution. The Rev. W. Jessop is governor and chaplain, and Mr. Henry M. Shera, LL.D., head master.

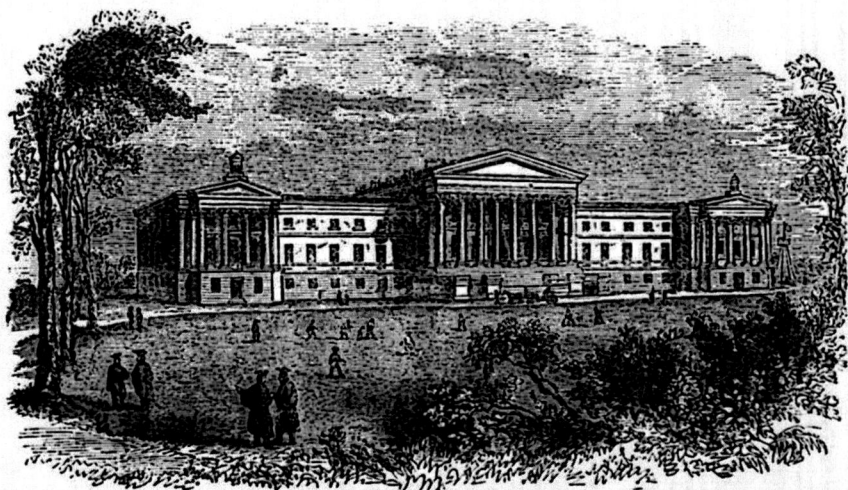

WESLEY COLLEGE.

THE GIRLS' HIGH SCHOOL.—In 1876, a committee of ladies and gentlemen interested in education was formed for the purpose of establishing a good high-class school for girls in Sheffield. This committee having entered into negotiations with the London Public Day School Company, secured the old Surrey-street Music Hall, as suitable premises for a school. The building, having been thoroughly renovated and adapted to school purposes, was opened as a Girls' High School in March, 1878. The head mistress is Mrs. Woodhouse (late of Clapham High School), who is assisted by a large staff of assistant mistresses and masters. The number of girls at the school in January, 1879, was 113. There is ample accommodation for 300 pupils. There are several scholarships open to pupils of this school, in common with those of the other schools in connection with the London Girls' Public Day School Company. The secretaries of the local committee are Mrs. W. Smith and the Rev. W. Moore Ede, M.A.

MECHANICS' INSTITUTION.—This Institution is carried on in a suite of rooms over the Council Hall and Free Library, in Surrey-street. Classes in the elementary branches of learning, and in French, chemistry, drawing, &c., are in operation. Students are prepared for examination under the Education Department, Whitehall; the Science and Art Department, South Kensington; and the Society of Arts. The Institution is managed by a committee of twenty members, Alderman Moore being president, and Mr. W. Armitage, secretary.

SCHOOL OF ART.—The history of the Sheffield School of Art is peculiarly interesting. The idea of establishing a " School of Design" (as these institutions were then entitled) was first mooted in Sheffield in 1841. A public meeting was called, but it was attended only by three individuals. Of this meeting, humble as it was, a record remains not to be surpassed for interest in the history of modern art in this country. Everybody remembers poor Haydon, the historical painter; his disgust at the success of Barnum's Tom Thumb, while his own historical paintings next door were almost unvisited ; his growing despair ; and his ultimate suicide. It happened that when the meeting was called in 1841, Haydon was in Sheffield, and, having a deep desire for the spread of his beloved art, he was one of the three persons who attended for the purpose of establishing the School. The other two were Dr. Harwood and Mr. H. P. Parker. During the progress of the "meeting" Haydon amused himself by drawing a pen-and-ink sketch of the persons present. This drawing has been framed, and may be seen at the Institution. Underneath the sketch are the following words in Haydon's writing, showing a latent humour in the painter's mind, the existence of which would hardly have been suspected :—" Public meeting at Sheffield, to establish a School of Design, October 13, 1841. Symptoms of great enthusiasm. Sketched by B. R. Haydon." Accompanying the sketch, also in Haydon's handwriting, is a transcript of the resolutions passed. An extract from these we give, on account of its proving so remarkably prophetic of the future of the institution :—" That, notwithstanding the neglect of the leading men of the town in not meeting, it is the duty of those who are assembled, amounting to *three*, to persevere till the great object be accomplished, aware from history that much greater revolutions have been begun and accomplished by much more incompetent means." Discouraging as this first attempt was, subsequent efforts were successful, and a School was opened in 1843, in Victoria-street, Glossop-road. The School was conducted with great success by Mr. Young Mitchell, who was appointed head master in 1846, and held the office until 1863, when failing health compelled him to resign. The foundation stone of the present building was laid by Dr. Branson on the 24th October, 1855, and it was opened in January, 1857. It is in Arundel-street, opposite the end of Surrey-street, is one of the most handsome and commodious educational structures in the town, and is

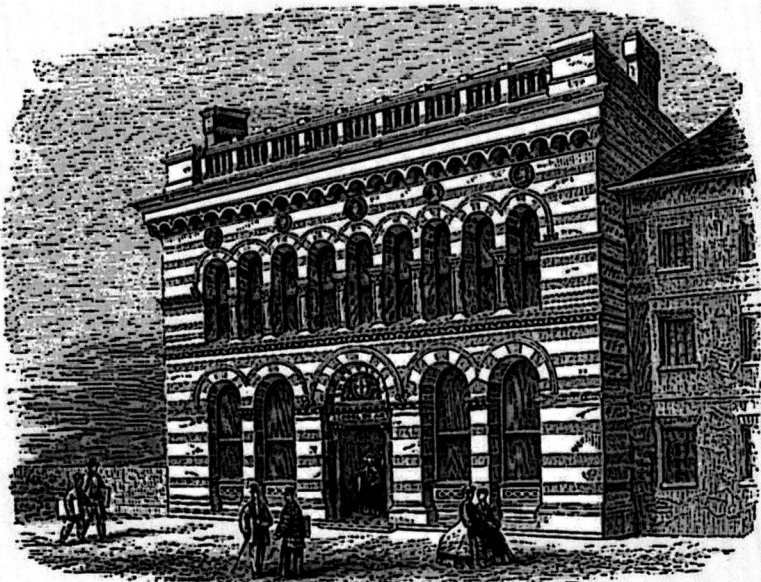

THE SCHOOL OF ART.

scarcely equalled by any other School of Art in the kingdom.
The architects were Messrs. Manning and Mew, of London,
and the total cost was about £7,000. The building covers
about 900 yards of land. It was erected in a most enterprizing
spirit, being adapted not merely to supply the existing wants of
the town, but to afford room for every possible expansion during
many years to come. The exterior appearance is striking and
handsome. It is a mixture of the Byzantine and Romanesque
styles. There are alternate layers of red and black brick, with
columns, &c., of stone. A debt of £1,500 was cleared off in
1868, through the exertions of Mr. Henry Wilson, of Sharrow,
and the building is now free from incumbrance. The condition
of the School as an educational institution fully corresponds with
the structure. The general position of the institution is in the
very first rank of the Schools of Art throughout the kingdom.
In 1869, it was placed at the head of our Art Schools by the
Department of Science and Art—the highest bonus of £50 being
awarded to the late Mr. Sounes, the then head master. Many
artists of great ability have been pupils at the School, including
the late Mr. Godfrey Sykes. Numerous valuable local prizes
are offered for competition by the pupils, including the Duke
of Norfolk's prize of twenty guineas, the Mayor's prize of ten

guineas, the Master Cutler's prize of five guineas, and two prizes of five guineas by Sir John Brown, &c. Mr. Wm. Cox is head master, and Mr. Arthur Wightman, hon. sec.

CHURCH OF ENGLAND EDUCATIONAL INSTITUTE.—This Institution, conducted as its name indicates on Church principles, takes high rank among evening educational institutions for the working classes. It was set on foot in 1840, but was carried on with comparatively little success until 1856, when it took a new start under the auspices of the Rev. James Moorhouse, now Bishop of Melbourne, and others of the clergy and laity, who came forward to assist the unpaid teachers who had borne the burden for so many years. The handsome building, in St. James'-street, of which we give an illustration, was opened in 1860, having been erected by public subscription. The Institution is still carried on with gratifying success. The subjects taught comprehend the Latin, German and French languages; natural theology; English literature; Euclid; book-

CHURCH OF ENGLAND EDUCATIONAL INSTITUTE.

keeping; singing, geography, English grammar and composition; reading, writing, arithmetic, &c. Classes for mathematics, chemistry, physical geography and applied mechanics are conducted in connection with the Department of Science and Art. The Rev. Canon Blakeney is president. There is a library in connection with the Institution.

YOUNG MEN'S CHRISTIAN ASSOCIATION.—This Society has rooms in Church-street, its object being to bring young men together for the purpose of imparting to them education of a religious tone. There are reading and class-rooms, and popular lectures are given during the winter in the Temperance Hall.

THE BOYS' AND GIRLS' CHARITY SCHOOLS.—The Boys' Charity School is at the north-east corner of the Parish Churchyard. It was founded in 1706 by Mr. Drake, the then vicar. The original School-house was built in 1710; the present School was erected in 1825. The principal benefactor of the School was Mr. Thos. Hanbey, the founder of Hanbey's Charity, whose portrait is preserved in the School. The income of the School is now considerable, and 100 poor boys are maintained and educated there. The Girls' Charity School is a kindred institution, and was formerly on the opposite side of the Churchyard, but in March, 1874, was removed to "Mount Pleasant," a large mansion at Highfield, built by Sir Francis Hart Sitwell towards the close of the last century; this house, with several acres of freehold land, were purchased and adapted by the trustees at a cost of about £5,500. The School was founded in 1786. Sixty girls are maintained, clothed, educated, and trained for domestic service. The School is mainly supported by subscriptions, the endowments being much smaller than those of the Boys' Charity School.

ROMAN CATHOLIC REFORMATORY.—The Roman Catholics have a Reformatory at Howard Hill, Steel-bank, for the reclamation of girls in the North of England who have fallen into crime. It was opened in August, 1861, and enlarged at a cost of about £1,700 in 1864. The institution is under the management of the Sisters of Charity of the Order of St. Joseph, and has accommodation for about 100 girls. There is a Roman Catholic Chapel in connection with the institution.

RANMOOR COLLEGE.—This institution was established for training young men for the ministry of the Methodist New Connexion. It is a handsome and imposing building in the Collegiate Gothic style of the fourteenth century, has a south

RANMOOR COLLEGE.

frontage of 212 feet, and stands conspicuously on the hill-side, to the right of Fulwood-road, a little beyond Ranmoor. The foundation stone of the College was laid September 25, 1862, by Mr. Mark Firth, and the College was opened in April, 1864. The building comprises a large centre hall, in which is the library, two lecture rooms, sixteen studios on the ground floor, with the same number of domitories over them, bath rooms and other conveniences. At the western end is the house for the governor and resident tutor. There is accommodation for six-teen students, and the building is arranged with a view to adding rooms for fourteen more, by an enlargement at the back. The site comprises about two acres of land, laid out in terraces and ornamental grounds. The College originated in this way. Mr. Thos. Firth, the father of Mr. Mark Firth, and the founder of the firm of Thomas Firth and Sons, left £5,000 towards the endowment of a College, on the condition that a further sum of £8,000 was raised. This was done; £3,000 being added to the endowment, leaving £5,000 for the land and buildings. A further sum had to be raised, however, the expenditure on the land and buildings being nearly £8,000. The Rev. W. Cocker, D.D., is principal, and the Rev. J. Stacey, D.D., classical tutor.

SURREY STREET EDUCATIONAL INSTITUTE.—This Institution, of which the late Mr. Chas. Wardlow was an indefatigable sup-porter, was established in 1844, its present premises in Surrey-street having been erected in 1862. It is carried on in connection with the United Methodist Free Churches, but is open to the general public. There are evening classes for instruction in elementary subjects, French, German, Drawing, &c.

ELEMENTARY EDUCATION IN SHEFFIELD.

THE SCHOOL BOARD.—The first School Board for Sheffield was elected on the 28th November, 1870. Special enquiries made shortly afterwards showed that there were nearly 40,000 children of school age in the borough and school accommodation for 28,000, but that only 12,000 children were actually attending school. The Board promptly adopted compulsory bye-laws, and, having hired temporary schools, proceeded to enforce attendance there and at the denominational schools. They also set themselves resolutely to the work of building new schools, being the first School Board in the kingdom to begin. The following table gives the number of schools completed to the end of last year, and the cost in round figures :—

SCHOOL.	Accommodation.	Size of Site in Square Yards.	Cost of Site.	Cost of Buildings and Fittings, including Caretakers' Houses where provided.	TOTAL COST.
			£	£	£
NEWHALL	664	2409	1546	5057	6603
BROOMHILL ...	326	2277	1151	3804	4956
NETHERTHORPE...	1015	3450	3016	8608	11624
PHILADELPHIA ...	1009	3895	3744	6661	10406
WALKLEY	773	3000	1080	7286	8366
CROOKESMOOR ...	835	2560	1790	8084	9870
LOWFIELD... ...	793	3055	2473	7225	9699
ATTERCLIFFE ...	794	2600	1254	7123	8377
CARBROOK	791	3000	1487	7578	9065
PYE BANK	902	3000	1139	8560	9699
PARK	787	2227	2561	7200	9761
DARNALL	753	2500	600	6195	6795
GRIMESTHORPE ...	813	3000	·857	7508	8365
SPRINGFIELD ...	833	2782	5047	10639	15686
MANOR	241	3000	602	5961	6564
FULWOOD	132	2722	262	1622	1885
	11461		28615*	109119*	137734*

* Shillings and pence omitted in the details are included in the totals.

The Board have purchased for £8,200 the Ragged and Industrial Schools, in Pea-croft, affording accommodation for 673 children, and have in progress five additional schools at Langsett-road, Heeley-bank, Brightside, Woodside, and Doctor's-fields, to accommodate 3,960, making a total of twenty-two sets of schools, with accommodation for 16,094 children, exclusive of temporary schools. At the close of last year, the Board had fifty-four school departments under its control and 320 paid teachers in its employ; they had 17,031 children, including half-timers, on the register, and the average attendance was 12,721. Through the action of the Board a very marked improvement had moreover been made in the attendance at voluntary schools. The total number on the rolls of Board and other efficient Elementary Schools was 45,727, the average attendance being 32,463, as compared with 12,000 when the Board began its work. In addition to ordinary subjects, girls are taught practical cookery and household work in the Board Schools; and in several of the infant schools Kindergarten instruction is carried on. Among other improvements in general education, the phonic system of teaching reading has been introduced. In connection with many of the schools penny banks have been opened, and night schools are conducted. The Board are establishing a " Truants' Industrial School " at Hollow Meadows, on the edge of the moors, a few miles from the town. The Board are erecting Central Schools, in which it is proposed to give higher instruction than can be given at the Elementary Schools to exceptionally clever scholars, to be selected by examination from the Elementary Schools, the education probably to include technical instruction bearing upon local industries. This is the first Board School of the kind projected, the Education Department having sanctioned it simply as an experiment in the direction of a more advanced education. It will provide accommodation for 240 senior boys, 244 senior girls, 230 junior boys and girls, and departments for 193 infants and forty-eight deaf and dumb children; total, 960.

BOARD SCHOOLS.

THE CENTRAL SCHOOLS AND OFFICES.—Avoiding a parsimonious economy, the School Board have erected substantial stone buildings on the best models, with distinctive architectural features. The schools are well arranged and are provided

CENTRAL BOARD SCHOOLS AND OFFICES.

with the best appliances. There is a playground, partly covered, to each school, and a caretaker's house. The Central Schools and Offices, of which we give an illustration, front upon the new street which is being made from Bow-street to Barker's-pool. The schools are arranged on the class-room system, with a large assembly hall in the centre for examinations and other such purposes. The offices comprise a large and hand-some Board room and adequate accommodation for a numerous and increasing staff of officers. The style of architecture of the offices and schools is the Renaissance, and, with the Firth College, they will be one of the finest ranges of buildings in the town. Sir John Brown has been chairman, and Mr. Firth, vice-chairman, of the Board from its constitution ; clerk, Mr. John F. Moss ; solicitor, Mr. Wm. Smith. The architects of the Central Schools and Offices are Mr. Robson, of London, and Mr. Flockton (Flockton and Gibbs). A majority of the district schools have been built from the designs of Messrs. Innocent and Brown.

THE FIRTH COLLEGE.—In close proximity to the Central Board Schools and Offices, and forming part of the same range of buildings, Mr. Mark Firth is erecting a very handsome block of buildings for lectures and classes, somewhat after the plan of those hitherto carried on in connection with the Cambridge University Extension movement. The University buildings are at the junction of the new street with Bow-street, and comprise large hall for lectures, and spacious class and other rooms. They will be vested in trustees ; the institution being managed by a council elected chiefly by the public bodies of the town. Provision is made in the scheme for the representa-tion of the Universities of Oxford, Cambridge, and London upon the Council, and it is probable that special privileges will be offered to successful students in the College by one or more of these Universities. The Council is to appoint a principal or rector in addition to such other professors as may be required to· carry out a system of higher education, both literary and scientific. It will also be empowered to accept gifts for the endowment of special chairs or professorships, or for the establishment of scholarships, under such arrangements as may be in harmony with the general design of the founder. Towards the endowment fund Mr. Samuel Roberts, M.A., J.P., of the Tower, Sheffield, has already offered a contribution of £1,000, and the Earnshaw Scholarships and the Firth Scholar-

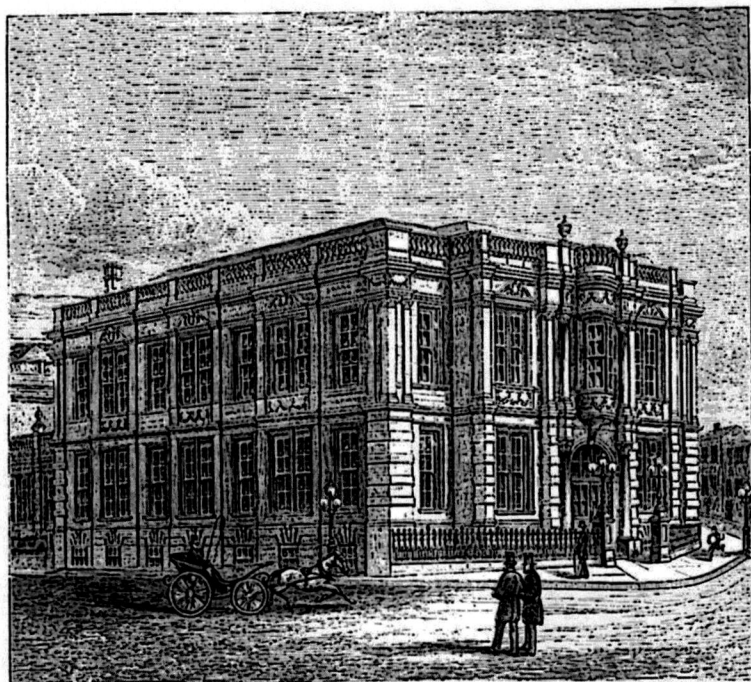

THE FIRTH COLLEGE.

ships will also be at once available in connection with the scheme. The estimated cost of the buildings is £20,000, and Mr. Firth has in addition offered a munificent sum towards an endowment fund to provide scholarships and exhibitions. The Firth College, as our illustration shows, is an exceedingly handsome building, in the same style of architecture as the Central Board Schools and Offices—namely, the Renaissance,—Messrs. Flockton and Robson being also the architects.

CHARITABLE INSTITUTIONS.

HE GENERAL INFIRMARY.—This noble institution, which is situated at the end of Shalesmoor, has been built and is sustained by public subscriptions and private bequests. The project of building an Infirmary was launched in April, 1792, at a public meeting called anonymously by Dr. Younge, a local physician. At first, owing to the magnitude of the effort required, it was languidly received; but some enthusiasm having been roused by the offer of £1,000 from Mrs. Fell, of Newhall, a sum of £15,000 was raised in a short time—£2,500 more being added before the building was finished. Thirty-one acres of land were purchased, "half-a-mile north-west of the town," as a suitable site; the first stone was laid in 1793, and the institution was opened October 4, 1797. Nearly the whole of the £17,500 having been expended on the land and buildings, the annual expenses had to be provided for by fresh subscriptions. Happily the institution had many benefactors; one anonymous contributor—afterwards found to be the Rev. Francis Gisborne, of Staveley—bequeathing £5,696 13s. 4d. A wing was added in 1840, at a cost of £6,000, for a fever ward; but doubts arising as to the wisdom of congregating infectious diseases within the building, it was ultimately appropriated to the general purposes of the institution. To meet the increased annual expenses much of the land, originally purchased in order to secure the institution "from the annoyance of manufactures and the too near approach of other buildings," was leased for building purposes, experience having shown that a town atmosphere was not unfavourable to town patients. In 1872-3, a detached wing, with rooms for forty beds, was erected and fitted up, at a cost of £12,000, for the treatment of offensive surgical cases and contagious diseases arising in the house. The General Infirmary is now a most efficient charity, accommodating and providing for 200 in-patients, and giving medicine and medical attendance to a much larger number of out-patients. Patients are admitted from the surrounding district, as well as from the town, on the recommendation of a subscriber. No recommendation is required in case of accident. In the Board room are busts of Dr. John Brown (the first chairman) by Chantrey; of

SHEFFIELD GENERAL INFIRMARY.

the Rev. James Wilkinson, by E. Smith (being a copy of the bust by Chantrey in the Parish Church); of Montgomery and Mr. Henry Jackson, by Ellis; of Mr. Thomas Rawson, by Law; and of Mr. Thomas Watson, of Broomfield. There are also portraits of several other persons of local celebrity.

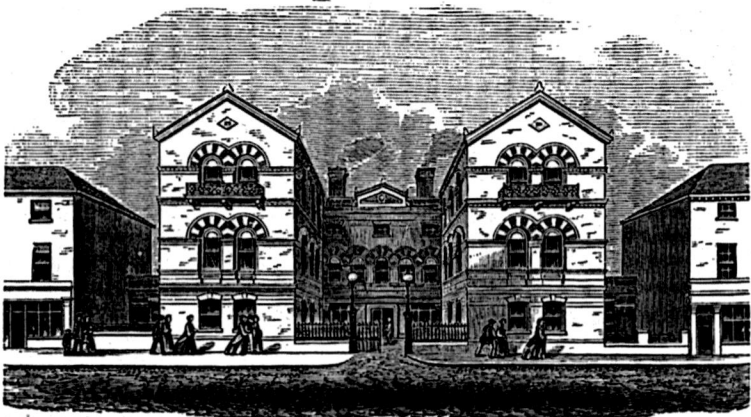

PUBLIC HOSPITAL AND DISPENSARY.—This institution was originally opened in Tudor-street in 1832 as a Medical Dispensary, and was removed to its present situation in West-street in 1833. In July, 1858, Earl Fitzwilliam laid the first stone of a new building on the old site, by which accommodation was provided for about fifty in-patients. In 1868 a front enlargement of the building was undertaken, and last year some much-needed structural improvements were effected, particularly in the culinary department. The Hospital has accommodation for 100 in-patients, and the Dispensary is carried on as vigorously and beneficially as when it was a separate institution. The Hospital and Dispensary has been erected and is supported by public subscription. The Rev. Henry H. Wright is chairman of the weekly board, and Mr. George F. Lockwood, honorary secretary.

THE JESSOP HOSPITAL FOR WOMEN. — A Hospital for Women was established in 1864 and carried on with success in Figtree-lane, but it has now been transferred to a splendid building in Upper Gell-street, near Brookhill, erected and furnished for the charity by Mr. Thomas Jessop, J.P. The new hospital was formally opened by Mr. Jessop in July of last year (1878). It is divided into two parts—one for the treatment of disease, and the other for midwifery. Practically there are two institutions under one roof, with distinct staffs and no internal communication. The entrance to the Hospital for Diseases is from Leavygreave-road, and in connection with it is a commodious department for out-patients, who enter from

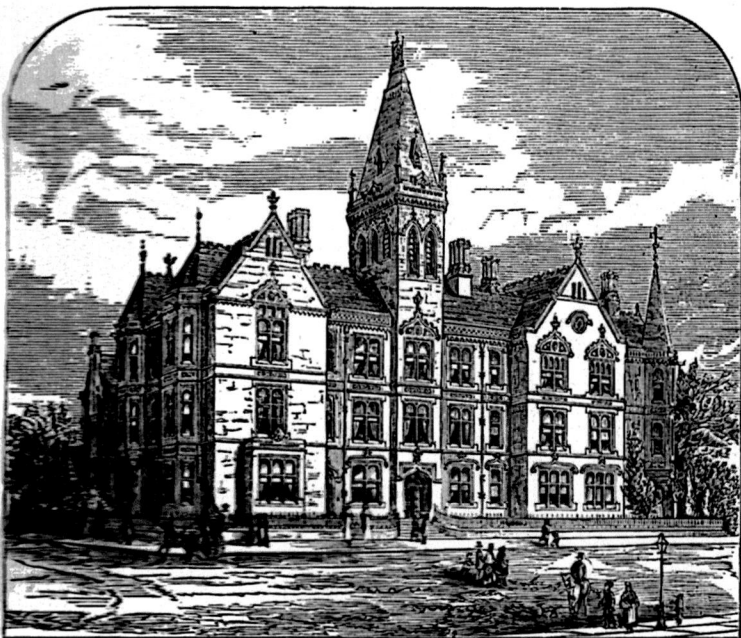

THE JESSOP HOSPITAL FOR WOMEN.

Gell-street and pass out into Leavygreave-road. The entrance
to the Midwifery Department is from Victoria-street. There
is provision in the two departments for sixty in-patients, and
for very complete medical and general staffs. The Hospital is
a three-storied building. The style is Tudor freely treated, the
architect, Mr. J. D. Webster, having introduced with very
good effect certain Burgundian features. The Hospital has
fine bay windows and a lofty tower, and is architecturally one
of the most successful public buildings in the town. It is
altogether a very noble structure, with spacious corridors, and
broad staircases. The rooms are large, airy and cheerful, and
are fitted and furnished in the best style without regard to cost,
the wards having beds and furniture of special designs and
quality, and floors of polished wainscot oak to avoid the damp
attendant on frequent washings. The institution, upon which
Mr. Jessop has generously expended over £26,000, has been
appropriately named the Jessop Hospital for Women. The
Hospital is supported by public subscriptions and donations.
Mr. Jarvis W. Barber, of George-street, is honorary secretary;
and Mr. Charles Warner, collector.

THE CHILDREN'S HOSPITAL.—This institution, which has been recently formed, has premises in Brookhill. It is for the special purpose of treating children under thirteen years of age suffering from accident or non-infectious diseases. The Hospital has accommodation for sixteen in-patients, and the medical officers already attend 120 to 130 out-patients daily. The charity is supported by subscriptions. The Rev. Canon Blakeney, vicar of Sheffield, is Chairman of the Board of Management, a committee of ladies investigating the circumstances of applicants. Dr. Cleaver is honorary secretary.

SHREWSBURY HOSPITAL.—This Hospital, which is opposite the Cholera Monument in Norfolk-road, was founded by direction of Gilbert, the seventh Earl of Shrewsbury, who died in 1616. The words of the will are:—"I will and appointe an hospitall to be founded at Sheffeilde for a perpetual maintenaunce of twentie poore personnes, and to be called 'The Hospital of Gilbert Erle of Shrewsbury,' and the same to be endowed with such revenues and possessions as my executors shall thincke fitt, not beinge under two hundred poundes a year." This direction was carried out by the Marquis of Newcastle as acting executor of the earl, notwithstanding some legal difficulties, and in 1665 the foundations of a hospital were laid on ground which had formerly been part of the orchard of the castle, and is now devoted to the new Corn Exchange. In 1673 the buildings were inhabited by ten men and ten women, and Mr. Henry Howard, who was great-grandson of Earl Gilbert, and in that year became Earl of Norwich and afterwards Duke of Norfolk, directed that the persons eligible to the charity should be poor " persons of good character of the town and parish of Sheffield, and if none such could be found there, of any other place or parish where he had estates that had descended to him from Gilbert, Earl of Shrewsbury, chosen by himself and his heirs." The inmates were to receive 2s. 6d. a week each, coals, and certain articles of dress ; and it was directed that they " should wear blue gowns and the master one of scarlet," and that they should " attend prayers read by the governor, and should be mutually assistant, pious, sober, and orderly in their conduct." The original hospital, standing near the Sheaf, was partially destroyed by a flood in 1768, four of the inmates being drowned. Edward, Duke of Norfolk, endowed the charity with a further sum of £1,000, which was applied in

SHREWSBURY HOSPITAL.

repairing the breach and enlarging the chapel. An Act having been obtained in 1823 for changing the site of the hospital, the present handsome buildings were erected in 1827 under the direction of Bernard Edward, Duke of Norfolk, who contributed £1,000 towards the cost. They include forty dwellings for the pensioners, a chaplain's house, and a chapel, on a site of 6a. 3r. 10p. The hospital accommodates twenty men and twenty women; the men receiving 14s., and the women 10s. 6d. a week each. The inmates have a load of coal each every three months, and an allowance of clothing every two years. The income of the charity is derived from property in Sheffield, Handsworth, Rotherham, Ecclesfield, Royston, Darfield, Penistone, and other places. The property has greatly increased in value. According to returns made to the Charity Commissioners, the accumulations in 1874 exceeded £50,000 and the revenue was over £11,000, while the amount expended upon the pensioners was less than £2,000. The allowances and list of out-pensioners have since been considerably increased. The Rev. John Stacye, M.A., is governor and chaplain, having been appointed in 1850. By his will, made in 1715, William Birley, of Throgmorton-street, London, left an endowment of £300 a year and a share of an estate at Neepsend to the governor of the hospital. The patronage of the hospital is vested in the Duke of Norfolk. An Act of Parliament obtained in 1725 provides that the governor of the hospital shall for ever be a clergyman of the Church of England.

MR. FIRTH'S ALMSHOUSES.—Among the best and noblest charities of the town are the Almshouses at Hanging-water, near Ranmoor, erected and endowed by Mr. Mark Firth, of Oakbrook, at a cost of £30,000. The first stone was laid by the Earl of Shaftesbury on the 4th March, 1869, and the Almshouses were opened during the following year. There are thirty-six houses, occupied by married couples or single persons, according to circumstances. They are in the form of a double quadrangle, the style being Early Gothic. In the centre is a chapel, with tower and spire, in the Early Decorated style. The chapel is pleasantly lighted by traceried windows of stained glass, the principal window being *in memoriam* of a daughter of the generous donor, who died in childhood. Each house has a living room and bedroom, with larder and coal cellar, and is supplied with gas and water. The allowance is 10s. a week to married couples and 7s. to single persons. The beneficiaries must be natives of Sheffield, of well-attested good character, and members of a Protestant church or congregation. Beside the chapel is a residence for the governor and chaplain. The property and endowments are vested in trustees for the benefit of the poor of Sheffield for ever. The Almshouses, with their lawn, flower beds and shrubberies, form a very handsome group, and are a most agreeable retreat for the aged and infirm who have been unfortunate in the battle of life.

THE LICENSED VICTUALLERS' ASYLUM.

THE LICENSED VICTUALLERS' ASYLUM.—The asylum for aged and decayed members of the Licensed Victuallers' Association and their wives or widows is opposite Dore station, in Abbeydale, about four miles from the town. The original Asylum was built at New Grimesthorpe in 1848, and for some years stood pleasantly among green fields; but after a time it was surrounded by manufactories, and became anything but a desirable retreat for the aged and the infirm. For the new asylum a very pleasant and salubrious situation has been selected. Having purchased five-and-a-half acres of land, with two houses upon it, at a cost of £6,000, the Association erected Asylum buildings at a cost of about £6,000 in 1878, the contract for the buildings, exclusive of boundary walls, &c., being £5,700. The Asylum consists of twelve houses, with a central hall for association meetings, library, &c. Each house comprises a living room, pantry, small bedroom for occasional use on the ground floor, and large bedroom upstairs. There is a broad lawn, with flower beds, in front of the building, and a separate kitchen garden for each house behind. The allowances to inmates are £32 10s. a year for married couples, and £22 2s. for single inmates. The Association do not restrict their benevolence to the support of inmates of the Asylum. They have numerous out-pensioners, to whom they make allowances of from 5s. to 10s. a week. The funds for the Asylum and out-pensioners are raised by annual subscriptions of members and honorary members of the Association, in addition to which there is an annual income of £150 from the two houses purchased as part of the estate. Mr. George Skinner, of Fitzwilliam-street, is secretary of the Association.

DEAKIN INSTITUTION.—This valuable charity was founded by Mr. Thomas Deakin, a Sheffield merchant, who died in 1849. Mr. Deakin bequeathed a sum of £3,000, the annual income to be applied for the benefit of unmarried women of good character, who should be "members of the Church of England or Protestant Dissenters acknowledging the Eternal Godhead of our Saviour as taught in the Church of England." He stipulated as a condition of the bequest that a further sum of £3,000 should be raised within two years from his decease. That sum having been subscribed, the charity was established in 1852 upon a scheme approved by the Master of the Rolls. The capital fund now amounts to nearly £30,000, and is yearly increasing. Donors of £50 become life governors, and subscribers of £5 5s. a year are governors after the third payment as long as the subscription is continued. The income is dispensed in annuities of £20 or £25, according to circumstances. Protestant women of straitened means, living in any part of England, who are at least forty years of age and have not been married, are eligible. Annuitants are elected at the annual meeting of the governors. Two admirable features in the management of the charity are these—privacy is observed in regard to annuitants, whose names are known only to the governors; and the Institution having neither offices nor paid officers, the whole of the income goes to the annuitants. The Archbishop of York is the president; Mr. J. H. Barber, of the Sheffield Banking Company, treasurer; and Mr. Arthur Thomas is the honorary secretary.

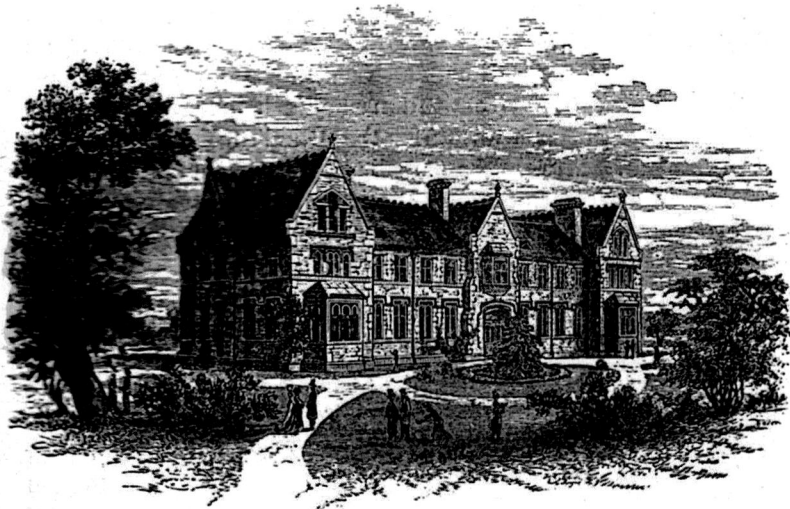

SCHOOL FOR THE BLIND.

SCHOOL AND MANUFACTORY FOR THE BLIND.—A Manufactory for the Blind was originated some years ago by the late Miss Harrison, of Weston. The premises are in West-street, and consist of a series of workshops at the back and a front shop for the sale of the goods made by the blind. About thirty blind persons, men and women, are constantly employed, receiving £600 to £700 a year in wages. The Manufactory is as nearly as possible self-supporting, the annual sales exceeding £2,300. Mat, rug, and brush making and chair caning are the chief employments. A missionary is employed to visit the blind in different parts of the town, and teach them to read and sew; and relief is given to the necessitous. By means of public subscriptions and donations the premises in West-street, which are freehold and have an area of 400 yards, have been purchased for the institution, and a sum of nearly £3,000 has been gradually accumulated for the rebuilding of the manufactory. A very handsome School for the Blind has been erected at Manchester-road, Broomhill, in the western suburbs. Mr. Daniel Holy, formerly of Burntstones, near Sheffield, who died in 1870, bequeathed the residue of his personal estate, amounting to about £20,000, to the Town Trustees upon trust (on the death of his sister, Mrs. Caroline Davenport), to pay the annual income to the treasurer for the support of a Blind

Institution. Mr. Holy attached to his bequest the condition that within five years after Mrs. Davenport's death a suitable building should be provided and furnished from other sources, and a request that the Institution should be conducted on the same plan as the Institution for the Blind at Edgbaston, near Birmingham. Mrs. Davenport died in 1875, and a public subscription for providing and furnishing the necessary buildings was begun shortly afterwards. The school is substantially built of stone. The principal entrance is in the centre, and divides the building into two wings—the right wing for boys and the left for girls. The wings have separate staircases in the centre, and side entrances to separate playgrounds. On the ground floor are dining and school-rooms, each 40 feet by 20 feet, work-rooms 30 feet by 20 feet, lavatories, committee rooms, matron's room, kitchens, pantries, &c. On the chamber floor are bedrooms, bath, lavatory, and sick rooms for each wing, and a nurses' room common to both; and there are attics in the roof for the servants. The grounds are about two acres in extent, mostly at the back of the buildings, and are laid out as playgrounds. The building is intended for the accommodation—to begin with—of twenty-five boys and twenty-five girls, but is capable of accommodating a greater number. It has been erected from the designs of Messrs. Flockton and Gibbs, and is a very handsome structure. It is well arranged, and the situation is all that could be desired. The cost of the building and site will be about £15,000, exclusive of furniture. The Earl of Wharncliffe is president, and Mr. W. R. Carter honorary secretary of the double institution.

HOLLIS' HOSPITAL.—This institution was founded by Thos. Hollis, who was apprenticed as a Sheffield cutler, but became a large hardware merchant in the Minories, London. Mr. Hollis was an earnest Dissenter of the Baptist persuasion and a liberal contributor to the first Dissenting meeting-house in Sheffield, opened in 1678, and called New Hall. After the erection of Upper Chapel, Norfolk-street, in 1700, Mr. Hollis purchased the disused New Hall Chapel, together with a small house adjoining, and converted them into dwelling-houses for sixteen elderly women, widows of cutlers and others employed in the peculiar manufactures of Sheffield. He supported the inmates during his life; and in 1726 his son Thomas vested Whirlow Hall estate, the fields through which Hollis-street was soon afterwards made, and other property in trustees for the benefit of the Hospital and assistance to Dissenting chapels and schools. The funds largely increasing, the Hospital, which is in New-hall-street, in the centre of the town, was rebuilt on the old site. The occupants receive 7s. a week each and an allowance of coals, &c. Connected with the Hospital is a day school attended by several hundred children, who pay 3d., 4d., or 6d. a week, according to the class they are in, the trustees providing school books. The governor, who is also schoolmaster, has a house and £60 a year, in addition to the school pence. The following annual payments are also made out of the trust :— To the minister of Upper Chapel, £30 ; of Nether Chapel, £10; of Fulwood Chapel, £20; of Rotherham Unitarian Chapel, £20 ; of Doncaster Chapel, £20 ; to a Doncaster schoolmaster, £20 ; and to the master of the schools in connection with the Rotherham Unitarian Chapel, £40. Mr. W. J. Sole is governor and schoolmaster at Sheffield, and Mr. Frederick Fowler is the receiver under the trust.

HANBEY'S CHARITY.—Mr. Thomas Hanbey, who died on Christmas Day, 1766, left £8,000 to the Cutlers' Company, upon trust, to apply the income of £3,000 to the maintenance and education of children in the Boys' Charity School, and to distribute the income of the remaining £5,000 among poor housekeepers in the parish, fifty years of age, of sober life and conversation, and members of the Church of England,—two-thirds of the recipients to be men,—the doles to be given yearly on the testator's birthday (July 29), and to consist of 20s. in money, a black hat, and a blue cloth coat or cloak. The kindred of the testator are always to have the preference in the selection of recipients, which is vested in the Cutlers' Company, the Church Burgesses, and the vicar and churchwardens of the Parish Church for the time being. Mr. Charles Younge (his nephew), the late Mr. Robert Younge, and the late Mrs. Matilda Ward have supplemented Mr. Hanbey's Charity by giving smaller sums to be distributed in a similar manner.

HADFIELD'S CHARITY.—Complying with the wishes of his deceased brother Samuel Hadfield, expressed shortly before his death, but not included in the provisions of his will, Mr. George Hadfield, of Manchester, by deed of gift dated May 23, 1850, vested £3,000 in the Cutlers' Company and the Mayor and Corporation, upon trust, to distribute the income among the poor of the town (not members of the Church of England), on the 28th of June each year, the object being to provide a similar Charity for those excluded from Hanbey's by reason of not being members of the Church of England.

WITHERS' PENSIONS. — Miss Sarah Withers, by her will dated November 15th, 1856, left £10,000, the income, after such deductions as might be required for keeping certain family monuments in St. Paul's church in repair, to be given in sums of £10 each to "widows or single women resident in the parish of Sheffield, in reduced, needy, or poor circumstances, of good character, sober life and conversation, members of the Church of England, incapacitated by illness or infirmity from earning their livelihood, or of the age of fifty years and never having received parochial relief." The pensioners are elected annually on the 26th October, being the birthday of Mr. Benjamin Withers, the testatrix's brother, in memory of whom the charity was established, the trustees having the option of electing the same pensioners from year to year. There are forty-six pensioners. The trustees are—the Incumbent of St. Paul's, Messrs. T. W. Rodgers, Charles Elliott, J. B. Mitchell-Withers, H. E. Watson, and H. I. Dixon. The trustees are to have an annual dinner after the election.

CHERRYTREE ORPHANAGE.—This charity derived its name from Cherrytree-hill, the suburban district where it originated. It has now eligible premises at Brook-hall, near Totley, about five miles from the town. There is a good stone house and several acres of land, which cost about £3,000. Orphan children are admitted from five to ten years of age, and a certificated teacher is employed to instruct them. Boys are apprenticed at the age of fourteen, and girls are trained for domestic service. The property is vested in trustees, and managed by a committee of Sheffield gentlemen, the household arrangements being under the charge of a ladies' committee. The institution is largely supported by voluntary contributions. Mr. David Ward, the mayor, is chairman; Mr. Wm. Howson, treasurer; Mr. W. K. Marples, honorary secretary; and Mr. William Hobbis, of Fitzwilliam-street, is assistant secretary and collector. This institution is open to orphans from all parts of the country.

SHEFFIELD ORPHANAGE.—A small Orphanage is carried on in Peacroft, in rooms formerly attached to the Ragged Schools, recently purchased by the School Board. A project is under consideration for establishing an Orphanage on the cottage plan, for Sheffield children exclusively, the sum of £8,200 given for the Ragged Schools to be applied to this purpose.

AGED FEMALE SOCIETY.—The object of this charity is to distribute money and clothing among poor and infirm women sixty-five years of age and upwards. A committee of ladies visit the poor and collect subscriptions. From £400 to £500 a year are distributed in sums of about 20s. Mr. Samuel Roberts, J.P., of Queen's Tower, is chairman of the society, and Mr. J. H. Barber, treasurer.

THE NURSES' HOME.—In 1871 a Nurses' Home was opened at 264, Glossop-road, for the purpose of training nurses to attend families in case of sickness. The institution is a very valuable one, and there is a constant demand for the very excellent nurses kept there. The institution is supported by donations and subscriptions. Mr. J. H. Barber is treasurer, and Mr. Jarvis W. Barber honorary secretary.

THE HOUNSFIELD PENSIONS.—Mr. George Hounsfield, who died at High Hazles in 1870, expressed a wish in his will that upon the death of his wife £20,000 should be vested in the Church Burgesses, the interest to be given yearly in pensions of £30 each, the pensioners to be men, unmarried women, or widows resident in England or Wales, members of the Established Church, in "reduced, needy, or poor circumstances," and not having received parish relief. Mrs. Hounsfield (now Mrs. Overend) directed that her deceased husband's wishes should be carried out at once, and the first election of pensioners took place on the 1st of July, 1870. There are nearly thirty pensioners, who are eligible for re-election from year to year.

OTHER CHARITIES.—The Overseers of Sheffield, Brightside, Ecclesall, and Nether Hallam are the trustees of small charities left from time to time, the income from which they distribute on St. Thomas' Day to aged widows and other poor people, but the amount altogether does not exceed £50 or £60, and it is mostly given away in small sums of 2s. 6d. to 5s. to each recipient.

The Church Burgesses distribute a small charity left by Mr. William Birley in 1715, one-third being paid, as already mentioned, to the Rev. John Stacye, M.A., chaplain of the

Shrewsbury Hospital; one-third to the master of the Free Writing School, who instructs 400 poor children, as free scholars, in writing and arithmetic, in a school belonging to the Church Burgesses; and the remaining one-third is distributed among the poor at Christmas, at the discretion of the same body.

There are two Schools in Ecclesall with small endowments, one at Sharrow-moor, and the other at Broad Oak-green. A sum of £5 a year, charged on land at Neepsend, is paid to the master of the former, who teaches twelve free scholars. In 1729, Thomas Marshall left the school-house at Broad Oak-green and 40s. a year for teaching six poor children to read English, and this is supplemented by the interest of £40 left by Robert Turie, clerk, for teaching six other poor children to read English and write. The Overseers of Ecclesall are trustees of these school charities.

SHEFFIELD WATERWORKS.

THE GREAT FLOOD.

SHEFFIELD was visited by a most appalling calamity in 1864, from the bursting of one of the large reservoirs constructed for the supply of the town with water. The Sheffield Waterworks are the property of a joint-stock company, bound under heavy penalties to provide adequately for the constantly increasing wants of the inhabitants, on terms regulated by Act of Parliament. Up to the early part of the fifteenth century the infant community was supplied mainly from a spring in the Ponds, and another near Westbar called "Bower Spring." In 1434 "Barker's Pool" was formed in Balm Green, then a pleasant suburb, and sufficed for more than two centuries. In 1713 pipes were laid to ponds and springs in Whitehouse-lane. Thirty years later artificial dams were made in the lower part of Crookesmoor valley, now let off in gardens. About 1782 the existing Damhouse reservoir was made, additional dams being constructed above it from time to time during the succeeding half-century. A Water Company was constituted in 1830 by Act of Parliament, with a capital of £100,000 and power to borrow £30,000. Having purchased the existing dams from Messrs. Matthewman and Battie, the previous owners, for £28,000, and the freehold of the land from the Duke of Norfolk for £4,000, the Company engaged Mr. J. Towlerton Leather as their engineer, and proceeded to extend their supplies. They completed the large service dam at Crookes in 1833, and soon afterwards constructed the middle and lower storage dams at Redmires. They also substituted iron mains for the primitive wood pipes, —made by boring through stems of young oak trees—hitherto used for the distribution of water. The compensation reservoirs in the Rivelin valley were next made, and in 1854 the large dam at Redmires was completed. Turning their attention to the Bradfield district, the Company next proceeded to construct a reservoir there for collecting the waters of a moorland stream known as Dale Dyke, completing it in the winter of 1863-4. The town having by this time become clamorous for the constant supply of water which the Company were bound by their last Act to give, the directors, in an evil hour, resolved to fill the new reservoir soon after it was finished. The Dale Dyke Reservoir, which covered 78 acres and contained nearly 700,000,000 cubic feet of water, was formed by throwing an embankment 1,200 feet long across the steep gorge of the stream. The embankment was nearly 100 feet high in the centre—a perilous height—and only 12 feet wide at the top; but it broadened to 500 feet in width at the base, and had the support of a central puddle-wall 19 feet thick. The engineers had, as they thought, demonstrated that it would resist ten times the pressure required of it, and no thought of danger was entertained. The large outlet pipes under the centre of the embankment having been closed, a heavy rainfall filled the dam rapidly, and a high wind, blowing down the gorge, hurled the water against the embankment in heavy waves. This was on the 11th March, 1864. During the afternoon Mr. Gunson, the resident engineer, made a careful inspection of the dam, and returned to Sheffield in the firm belief that all was safe. An hour later a labourer crossing the embankment noticed a horizontal crack in the outer slope and reported it to the contractor, who, as no water came through, thought it was a mere frost crack, but nevertheless opened the outlet pipes and sent his son on horseback for Mr. Gunson. The saddle-girth breaking, the youth pulled up for repairs at the little hamlet of Damflask, two miles below, and told of the crack. Labourers and villagers hurried up, and in the darkness anxiously examined the crack with lanterns. At first they made light of it; but by the time Mr. Gunson arrived—(10 o'clock) — the appearances had become alarming, and he attempted to let off the water by blowing up the waste weir with gunpowder. The first attempt failed. Before a second could be made the centre of the embankment yielded, and the liberated waters, descending the steep and narrow gorge of Dale Dyke in a cataract to Low Bradfield, swept like an avalanche down the course of the river Loxley to Hillsborough, and down the Don through the town, deluging the valleys on both sides to the depth of many feet. In the higher parts of the Loxley valley the depth of water must have been from twenty to thirty feet, and it swept all before it. In the wider valley of the Don, at Owlerton and Neepsend, it was high enough to cover many of the lower houses, and float beds and furniture in the upper rooms of others, and to tear up and carry away huge boilers, beams, and wreck of all kinds. Even in the Wicker, it was sufficiently high to run over the parapet of Lady's Bridge and flood the streets and houses to the depth of four or five feet.

It was midnight when the flood broke its barriers. At Low Bradfield the people were astir and escaped up the hill-side on hearing the distant roar. They saw with horror their strong stone bridge, flour mill, schools and other buildings disappear like sand-hills before the advancing tide. The destruction at Damflask, the next hamlet, was similar. The bridge, the inn, and other houses were swept away, but the occupants, having also been forewarned, were astir and escaped. At each hamlet, however, the flood claimed one victim. At Bradfield the fringe of the flood struck the village tailor as he hurried away with his helpless wife and newly-born infant, washing the child out of its mother's arms. At Damflask the victim was an excavator, who, having examined the crack, went to bed scoffing at the idea of danger. He was found buried in debris far down the valley next day. Below Damflask no hint of danger had penetrated, and the few scores of men and boys on "night shift" at the works were almost the only persons astir. Upon them in the darkness the deluge came as a terrible surprise, sweeping away many of the works, and overwhelming the workers in their bewildered attempts to escape. In the populous district below "Little Matlock" the destruction and loss of life was awful, whole families being swept away, either unconsciously in their beds or clinging convulsively together in groups, shrieking for help which none could give. Farmer Trickett, with his wife, children, servants, father-in-law, and a gentleman lodger, occupied a substantial stone house at the junction of the Loxley and the Rivelin. A neighbour on the hill-side saw the foaming torrent approach "like a mountain of snow" and strike the house so heavily that it rocked like a cradle. Lights flickered in the windows, and shrieks were heard, as the house sank beneath the flood, not a wreck remaining nor a soul escaping. Fifteen adjacent cottages—two whole rows—were similarly swept away. Only three of their seventy inhabitants survived — two young men who drifted safely across the torrent in their bed and landed in a neighbouring field, and William Watson, who, having been carried away with his wife and family, was tossed upon a heap of debris against the house of a neighbour, who drew him naked and exhausted through the bedroom window. Other houses were struck obliquely and only half destroyed, all the inmates being taken in some cases, and a few being left in others. Here and there a courageous father, like Thomas Chapman at Little Matlock, and William Whittles at Hillbridge, succeeded in rescuing all, or nearly all their family from the very jaws of death by huddling them together in a corner and clinging tenaciously to the fragment of their ruined homes until the danger was past. Scenes of death and destruction, of which these are but examples, occurred all along the Loxley valley from Bradfield and Damflask to Malin Bridge and Hillsborough, and the scenes in the valley of the Don at Owlerton and Sheffield were scarcely less harrowing. At Bacon Island for instance, William Wright, his wife and a little visitor were carried away with the gable of the house, their own child being found after the flood had passed softly sleeping in its bed, the candle lighted by its lost parents still burning near. At Neepsend, widow Bright, with a son, two grand-children and a lodger perished in a group after part of the house had gone; a grandson who scrambled up the chimney alone escaping. Near them was a low white-washed cottage occupied by an Irish labourer named Gannon, his wife and six young children. They all got upon the slates, but the flood rose relentlessly and lifted off the roof, carrying them all away. Among those who perished in the town were many occupants of ground floor rooms and one-story houses. Some of these, including two aged invalids and three children whose parents were away at a funeral, were drowned in their sleep; but others had evidently been roused and battled agonizingly with the flood as it gradually filled the room and smothered them in its cold embrace. Those whose houses were in the fringe of the flood escaped half naked to the Town Hall and other places of refuge, some few perishing in the attempt; but to thousands flight was impossible, and their alarm was terrible. The torrent came suddenly: its cause and limits were unknown; loaded with wreck of all kinds, it thundered against doors and walls like a battering ram, and it rose rapidly. Happily it passed in a brief half-hour, carrying many of its victims miles down the valley towards Doncaster, and leaving behind it a scene of death and wreck and desolation almost unparalleled in the annals of English towns, though vastly exceeded by the recent disaster in Hungary. The number of dwellings flooded was 4,511, of which 39 were wholly and 376 partially destroyed. Many persons were injured, and though the hair-breadth escapes were numerous and in many cases almost miraculous, 240 lives were sacrificed. The destruction of manufactories and property of all kinds was enormous.

In response to the appeal of Mr. Thomas Jessop, J.P., the mayor, a sum of £55,214 was promptly subscribed, being more than sufficient to meet urgent claims. The liability of the Water Company was established, and the amount they ultimately paid was—For loss of life, £9,080 7s. 11d.; personal injury, £4,993 4s. 5d.; damage to property and trade, £262,844 19s. 3¾d., making a total of £276,918 11s. 7¾d., exclusive of an enormous sum in law and other expenses, and the heavy cost of new dams. The Company were fortunate in the parliamentary campaign which necessarily followed the calamity. They were authorised to add 25 per cent. to their water rents for twenty-five years, and to borrow £400,000, in order to meet their liabilities and complete their system of works.

The cause of the disaster was the subject of much contention, and was never satisfactorily ascertained. The coroner's jury,* after hearing much scientific evidence, were of opinion that "there had not been that engineering skill in the construction of the works which their magnitude and importance demanded." Five eminent engineers, subsequently employed by the Company to report, attributed the calamity to a landslip on the east side of the embankment, extending under a portion of the outer slope.

Since the flood the Company have completed the Agden dam, then in course of construction, near Bradfield. They have constructed a new Dale Dyke reservoir near the site of the broken one, and higher up the same valley have made the Strines reservoir. In the Loxley valley, nearer Sheffield, on the site of the destroyed village of Damflask, they have made their largest reservoir.

* The members of the jury were:—Mr. John Webster, coroner; Mr. W. W. Woodhead, deputy coroner; Mr. Henry Pawson, foreman; Messrs. T. Prideaux, J. B. Fordham, J. Walker, C. G. Porter, Hy. Pearce, T. Appleyard, Thos. Howson, John Bland, R. Booth, S. Dawson, F. W. Colley, Thos. W. Cole, Fredk. J. Mercer, E. Bennett, and Wm. Marples. The Town Clerk, Mr. John Yeomans, was also present during the inquest.

The following is a list of reservoirs, with the number of acres they cover, and the cubic feet of water they will hold :—

	ACRES.	CUBIC FEET OF WATER.
Old Dam, Crookesmoor ...	13	8,000,000
Crookes Dam ...	4¾	3,500,000
Middle Redmires ...	48	30,000,000
Lower do. ...	28¾	22,000,000
Upper do. ...	56	55,000,000
Lower Rivelin ...	29½	28,750,000
Upper do.	10¾	8,000,000
Agden	65	91,000,000
Dale Dyke	75	114,000,000
Strines	50	67,000,000
Damflask	112	128,000,000
	492¾	554,250,000

This enormous storage is rendered necessary by the Company being under an obligation to send seven cubic feet per second down the Rivelin, and ten cubic feet per second down the Loxley—1,020 cubic feet per hour—during the longest drought of a dry summer as compensation to the millowners on those streams. With this large deduction, the storage is in excess of all possible wants of the town for some time to come, and the Damflask reservoir has not yet been filled.

SHEFFIELD CELEBRITIES.

OUR notice of eminent Sheffield men, whose names stand prominently out in connection with history, literature, science and art, must be confined to a few lines.

James Montgomery, the poet, was born at Irvine, in Ayrshire, in November, 1770, and educated at Fulnec school. He was the son of a Moravian minister, and intended for the same calling, but the idea was abandoned, and he was placed in a retail shop at Mirfield, near Wakefield. Running away from Mirfield eighteen months afterwards, he took a similar situation at Wath, near Rotherham. In 1790, he tried his fortune in London, but without success, and returned to Wath, remaining there until 1792, when he obtained employment as literary assistant to Mr. Gales, the proprietor of the *Sheffield Register*, afterwards named the *Iris*. Two years later Mr. Gales quitted the country for political reasons, leaving Montgomery to manage the newspaper for his sisters. This was in the troublous times which succeeded the French Revolution, and Montgomery was twice fined and imprisoned. In 1794 he was fined £20 and imprisoned three months for printing a harmless ballad, declared to be seditious. In 1795, when he had become proprietor of the paper, he was prosecuted by Colonel Athorpe for libel, fined £30 and imprisoned six months. The volunteers of that day having been called out to quell a riot, fired upon the crowd in obedience to the orders of Colonel Athorpe, killing two men and wounding others. In describing what followed in the *Iris*, Montgomery said : — "A person, who shall be nameless, plunged with his horse among the unarmed, defenceless people, and wounded with his sword men, women and children promiscuously." This was the libel for which, though substantially true, Montgomery was so severely punished. His paper afterwards prospered, yielding him a handsome competence and leisure for the poetic pursuits for which he had shown a taste as a youth. The Government of Sir R. Peel moreover gave him a pension for

THE HARTSHEAD—FROM A SKETCH IN 1862,

SHOWING THE SHOP AND OFFICE AT WHICH THE POET MONTGOMERY WROTE AND

PUBLISHED "THE IRIS" AND MOST OF HIS POETICAL WORKS.

life of £200 a year. Montgomery's principal poems were "The Wanderer of Switzerland," published in 1806; "The West Indies," "The World before the Flood," and "The Pelican Island;" but he was the author of many smaller pieces and many beautiful hymns. He died at The Mount, April 30th, 1854; his interment at the General Cemetery being the occasion of a great public demonstration. To the monument erected over his grave we have already alluded; and we give an illustration of the house in Hartshead, in the centre of the town, where he published his newspaper and wrote the greater part of his poems. The house is still standing, though much of the old property surrounding it has disappeared. It is opposite to the new offices erected for the Town Clerk.

DARFIELD CHURCH.

Ebenezer Elliott, the "Corn-Law Rhymer" and poet, was born at Masbrough, near Rotherham, in 1781, his father being employed at the Masbrough Iron Works. Elliott worked with his father up to manhood; afterwards started in business at Rotherham and failed, and then came to Sheffield and began in the steel trade with £100, his house and place of business being at the corner of Burgess-street and Barker's-pool, where the Albert Hall now stands. In 1833, Elliott took a more commodious steel warehouse in Gibraltar - street, between the bottom of Trinity-street and Snow-hill, building himself a house at Upperthorpe. Speaking of his years of struggle, the poet said—"I had to rock the cradle and stir the melted butter while I wrote my poetry. The poetry was spoilt and the melted butter was burnt." Eventually Elliott made his way to independence, retiring with £6,000. The trenchant "Corn-Law Rhymes" which first made him famous are now little read, but some of his descriptive and lyrical poems are among the finest in the language, and are enduring monuments of his poetic genius. Elliott passed the closing years of his life at the village of Great Houghton, near Barnsley. He died on the 1st December, 1849, and was buried in Darfield churchyard. This fine old village church, of which we give an illustration, is beautifully situated on the brow of a gentle acclivity immediately beyond Darfield station, on the Midland railway, fourteen miles north of Sheffield. Its burial ground is a fitting resting place for so passionate a lover of nature. Elliott's monument, previously described, is in Weston Park ; and there is a good portrait of him at the Mechanics' Institution, in Surrey-street.

The Rev. Joseph Hunter, the learned historian of "Hallamshire" and of the "Deanery of Doncaster," was born in Sheffield in 1783. He was a Unitarian Minister in early life, but was afterwards appointed one of the Vice-keepers of the National Records. He died in 1861, and was buried at Ecclesfield. Ebenezer Rhodes, the author of "Peak Scenery," a beautiful work, illustrated with engravings from drawings by Sir Francis Chantrey, was a Sheffield manufacturer, and Master Cutler in 1808. There are portraits of both these writers in the Cutlers' Hall. Mr. John Holland, of whom there is a bust in the Cutlers' Hall, was curator of the Literary and Philosophical Society for many years, and a voluminous writer in prose and verse. He was a native of Sheffield, and the friend and biographer of Montgomery. He also published a life of Chantrey. Mr. Holland died on the 28th December, 1872, aged 78 years. Mr. Samuel Bailey, whom Elliott styles "The Bentham of Hallamshire," had an almost European reputation as a philosophic writer. He amassed a fortune in early life in manufacturing pursuits, and died on the 18th January, 1870, leaving £80,000 to the Town Trustees for public uses. He also was a native of the town, and lived to an advanced age. Neither Montgomery nor Holland, nor Bailey married. Contemporary with these were Mr. Samuel Roberts, of Queen's Tower, Mrs. Hofland, Dr. Geo. C. Holland and others of literary fame, whose writings helped to give a tone to Sheffield society during the first half of the present century.

Of Sir Francis Chantrey, R.A., the greatest English sculptor, Sheffield has especial reason to be proud. He was born on the 7th April, 1781, at the village of Norton, where his father had a small farm. In his boyhood, Chantrey for a time brought milk to Sheffield daily, and is thus described by Elliott :—

"Calmly seated on his panniered ass,
Where travellers hear the steel hiss as they pass,
A milkboy, sheltering from the transient storm,
Chalked on the grinder's walls an infant form."

THE BIRTHPLACE OF CHANTREY.

Showing a taste for art, Chantrey was apprenticed at an early age to Mr. Robert Ramsay, a carver and gilder in High-street, Sheffield. His indentures were cancelled after a few years, and he went to London for study. During a short stay in Sheffield, in 1802, he very modestly advertised in the *Iris* for employment, "in taking portraits in crayons and miniatures." During the recess of the Royal Academy in 1804, he "solicited the patronage of the ladies and gentlemen of Sheffield and its environs," in "sculpture and portrait painting." His first work in marble, executed in 1806, was a bust of the Rev. James Wilkinson, a late vicar of Sheffield, and the remarkable success he achieved in this first effort determined his career. Chantrey, who was knighted by William IV., died in London on the 25th Nov., 1841. He was buried in accordance with his own wishes, in the churchyard at Norton, where are memorials of him, described in our account of the place. Chantrey left directions in his will that, so long as his tomb was preserved, £50 a year should be paid out of his estate for the education of ten poor boys at Norton, and £10 a year each to ten poor old people, five of each sex. Among the works of the great sculptor preserved in the town are the following: in the Parish Church, the bust of the Rev. James Wilkinson, and a memorial of Mr. and Mrs. Harrison, of Weston; in St. Paul's Church, a memorial of the Rev. A. Mackenzie; at the Infirmary, two stone figures, being his first essay with the chisel, and a bust of Dr. Browne; at the Cutlers' Hall, four casts. These works are referred to in detail in our descriptions of the buildings.

There are memorials by Chantrey of Mrs. Cooke, in Owston Church, near Doncaster; and of the late Sir Richard Arkwright, in Cromford Church; and a monumental group in Ilam Church, Dovedale, rivals in interest his "Sleeping Beauties" in Lichfield Cathedral and other great works. Sheffield can boast of several other sculptors of more than local reputation, and is worthily represented in painting by the late Thomas Creswick, R.A., and by Hawksworth, McIntyre, Poole, Pigott, Richard Smith, &c.

Sheffield can also boast of numbering among her departed sons a great composer. Sir William Sterndale Bennett was born in 1816; his father, who was organist of the Parish Church, died a few years afterwards, and the infant musician was educated by his grandfather, who lived at Cambridge. His musical career was an uninterrupted success. He was appointed Principal of the Royal Academy of Music in 1868. He was knighted on the 24th of March, 1874, but did not long live to enjoy this distinction. The marble bust of the deceased in the old dining room at the Cutlers' Hall was provided by public subscription, and unveiled in December, 1875. It was executed by Mr. L. A. Malamprié, of London, and bears the following inscription:— "Sir William Sterndale Bennett, M.A., Mus. Doc., D.C.L., Professor of Music in the University of Cambridge, and Principal of the Royal Academy of Music, born at Sheffield, April 13th, 1816; died February 1st, 1875. Interred at Westminster Abbey."

In science Sheffield is not less worthily represented by Mr. Henry Clifton Sorby, who is happily still living and active. Mr. Sorby was born at Woodburn, Attercliffe, on the 10th May, 1826, his father, Mr. Henry Sorby, who married Miss Lambert, of London, being a member of the old and well-known firm of J. and H. Sorby, of Spital-hill, edge tool manufacturers. Mr. H. C. Sorby was educated at the Collegiate School, Sheffield, and by private masters, and showed a taste for scientific pursuits as a youth. Enjoying a happy immunity from the cares of business, Mr. Sorby was impressed with the importance of making his life a useful one, and devoted himself to the study of geology and other branches of science, with an ardour which has made him as eminent in the scientific world as Sir Francis Chantrey was in the world of art. More than a hundred memoirs on various subjects from his pen have appeared from time to time in leading scientific journals. The four subjects on which he has chiefly written are: the application of the microscope to the study of the structure of rocks; the application of spectrum analysis to investigations with the microscope; the structures produced by currents in stratified rocks; and a new optical method of identifying minerals. Mr. Sorby was the first to apply the microscope to the examination of rock structure. It was a new method of investigation, and is throwing a flood of light on the science of geology. Not less important is the application of the spectrum microscope to the examination of animal and vegetable colouring matter, and to the detection of blood stains found in criminal investigations. Pursuing his new methods, Mr. Sorby was the first to prove the direct correlation between mechanical forces and chemical action in the Bakerian lecture for 1863. He first gave a satisfactory explanation of the origin of the cleavage of slate rocks. His presidential address to the Geological Society of London this year was on the " Structure and Origin of Limestone "—a subject upon which he had been engaged more than thirty years. The great value of Mr. Sorby's discoveries is not unrecognized by the scientific world. The Wollaston Medal of the Geographical Society was awarded to him in 1869 for the application of the microscope to the structure of rocks and minerals. In 1872 he received the Boerhaave Medal of the Dutch Society of Sciences—a large gold medal given once in twenty years to the investigator who is judged to have done the most to advance our knowledge of mineralogy and geology during the preceding twenty years. In 1874 Mr. Sorby received the large gold medal given by Her Majesty, awarded by the Royal Society—the most ancient and eminent scientific Society in the world—in recognition of the great importance of his discoveries in the application of the microscope to mineralogy and geology, and of the spectrum microscope to the investigation of animal and vegetable colouring matter. Mr. Sorby is a Fellow of the Royal Society, and President of the Geological Society of London, of the Mineralogical Society, of the Yorkshire Naturalists' Union, and of the Sheffield Literary and Philosophical Society. He has been elected honorary or corresponding member of various other scientific societies— not only in this country but on the continent and in the United States of America. His authority among scientific men is world-wide, and Sheffield never had a son of whom she was more justly proud. The medals awarded to Mr. Sorby are deposited in the Weston Museum.

The Rev. Samuel Earnshaw, M.A., of Sheffield, is also well known in the educational and scientific world. He was the Senior Wrangler of the his year at Cambridge, and has published a considerable number of original mathematical works, showing his investigations in dynamics, optics, and acoustics.

IRON AND STEEL—CRUDE AND MANUFACTURED.